THE AMBIVALENCES OF RATIONALITY

Is rationality a well-defined human universal, such that ideas and behaviour can everywhere be judged by a single set of criteria? Or are the rational and the irrational simply cultural constructs? This study provides an alternative to both options. The universalist thesis underestimates the variety found in sound human reasonings exemplified across time and space and often displays a marked Eurocentric bias. The extreme relativist faces the danger of concluding that we are all locked into mutually unintelligible universes. These problems are worse when certain concepts, often inherited from ancient Greek thought, especially binaries such as Nature and Culture, or the literal and the metaphorical, are not examined critically. Drawing on a variety of disciplines, from philosophy to cognitive science, this book explores what both ancient societies (Greece and China especially) and modern ones (as revealed by ethnography) can teach us concerning the heterogeneity of what can be called rational.

G. E. R. LLOYD is Emeritus Professor of Ancient Philosophy and Science in the University of Cambridge, former Master of Darwin College, Cambridge, and Senior Scholar in Residence at the Needham Research Institute, Cambridge. He has held Visiting Professorships in Europe, North America, the Far East and Australasia. He is the author of twenty-three books and editor of a further five. He won the Sarton Medal for History of Science in 1987, the Kenyon Medal for Classical Studies in 2007, the Dan David prize in 2013 and the Fyssen prize in 2014, and he was knighted for services to the history of thought in 1997.

THE AMBIVALENCES OF RATIONALITY

Ancient and Modern Cross-Cultural Explorations

G. E. R. LLOYD

Needham Research Institute, Cambridge

CAMBRIDGE
UNIVERSITY PRESS

CAMBRIDGE
UNIVERSITY PRESS

University Printing House, Cambridge CB2 8BS, United Kingdom

One Liberty Plaza, 20th Floor, New York, NY 10006, USA

477 Williamstown Road, Port Melbourne, VIC 3207, Australia

314–321, 3rd Floor, Plot 3, Splendor Forum, Jasola District Centre, New Delhi - 110025, India

79 Anson Road, #06-04/06, Singapore 079906

Cambridge University Press is part of the University of Cambridge.

It furthers the University's mission by disseminating knowledge in the pursuit of
education, learning, and research at the highest international levels of excellence.

www.cambridge.org
Information on this title: www.cambridge.org/9781108420044
DOI: 10.1017/9781108328951

© G. E. R. Lloyd 2018

First published 2018

Printed in the United Kingdom by Clays, St Ives plc

A catalogue record for this publication is available from the British Library

ISBN 978-1-108-42004-4 Hardback

Deux excès: exclure la raison, n'admettre que la raison
(*Two Excesses: To Exclude Reason; To Allow Reason Alone*)
Blaise Pascal, *Pensées* 253 (Brunschvicg)

Contents

Acknowledgements

This book largely stems from conversations and exchanges that I have had the good fortune to have with a series of interlocutors, specialists in a considerable variety of fields, over the past half-dozen years. In some cases my friendship with those interlocutors goes back several decades. In others my acquaintance is much more recent, dating from encounters at conferences, or correspondence that followed from occasions when I have reviewed their books or they reviewed mine. I have the editors of the *Journal of the Royal Anthropological Institute*, of *Interdisciplinary Science Reviews*, and of *HAU* to thank for several of those. Based at the Needham Research Institute at Cambridge, and associated with two colleges, Darwin and King's, with the Centre for Research in the Arts, Social Sciences and Humanities, and with several different faculties, including especially of course Classics and the History and Philosophy of Science, I have been in the fortunate position of being able to benefit from the advice of colleagues across the widest possible spectrum of disciplines and not just, of course, here at Cambridge.

The initial stimulus to focus on rationality came from interactions with my colleagues in Classics, Myles Burnyeat, Renaud Gagné, Simon Goldhill, Malcolm Schofield, David Sedley, Tim Whitmarsh, and especially from a sequence of exchanges with Gabor Betegh and Robert Wardy. The social anthropologists with whom I have interacted include Manuela Carneiro da Cunha, Philippe Descola, Elisabeth Hsu, Stephen Hugh-Jones, Caroline Humphrey, Tanya Luhrmann, Anastasia Piliavsky, Marilyn Strathern, Aparecida Vilaça and Eduardo Viveiros de Castro. I have learnt much from dialogues with those who share the ambition to combine history with philosophy of science, notably Hasok Chang, Nick Jardine, Chessie Rochberg and Liba Taub. Although I am no computer programmer I have benefited from conversations on the problems of artificial intelligence with Alan Blackwell and Willard McCarty. My sinologist friends under the leadership of Mei Jianjun at the Needham Research Institute and of Roel Sterckx at the Faculty of Asian and Middle Eastern Studies have saved me from many mistakes, as have other long-standing advisers, Karine Chemla, Anne Cheng, Liu Dun, Michael Loewe, Michael Nylan, Nathan Sivin especially. Nor should I fail to mention less senior scholars who have recently pursued comparative studies in a variety of fields with interesting results that bear on the problems of rationality: Xiaofan Amy Li, Xinyi Liu and Jingyi Jenny Zhao especially. Preliminary statements of some of my arguments here have been presented as lectures at Berlin, Berne, Rome and Malta, and thanks go to Markham Geller, Richard King, Lorenzo Perilli and Paul Sant Cassia for those invitations. Finally, I have once again the staff at Cambridge University Press and my editor, Michael Sharp, to thank for their expert advice and support.

CHAPTER I

Aims and Methods

A major preoccupation that has been with me ever since I began research on ancient Greece has been the question of the varieties of human thought and reasoning. To what extent, indeed, is it correct to say that thought and reasoning – that is, the faculties themselves, as opposed to the products of their exercise – exhibit differences? Are the differences we might identify merely superficial or surface appearances overlying fundamental constancies? In which case, can we characterise those constancies – thereby pinning down what we may consider to be basic to all human thought and reasoning? Or do we have to say that no such constancies exist? Spreading the net wider, how does human reasoning relate to the intelligent behaviour we can recognise in other species of animals, or, come to that, to what we customarily label 'artificial intelligence'?

If we accept, as we surely must, that argument, persuasion and debate play a massive role in reasoning, how does the social context of such activities influence the modes of reasoning we deploy, and can that be used to differentiate human reasoning from those other kinds as well as to chart differences within different modes of human reasoning? Some might suppose that our thoughts and attitudes are determined by who we are, the social roles we play, even the language we speak. Even those who would object that 'determined' is too strong a term are likely to accept that such factors do indeed at least influence those thoughts and attitudes. Can we, then, pinpoint the extent of such influences and conversely the room for manoeuvre and criticism that remains?

The questions are easy enough to formulate, but it is not at all easy to say how we can begin to hope to answer them. If we accept that we bring to any inquiry a set of presuppositions and assumptions that reflect our personal histories, we must evidently endeavour, in the first instance, to the best of our ability, to identify and scrutinise them. We must grant that we deploy some more or less circumscribed set of concepts and categories but at the same time allow, indeed insist – for this is a crucial point – that they are provisional and revisable. Access to others' modes of reasoning and thought provides a particular challenge but can be especially rewarding in introducing us to assumptions that differ from our own, leading us, sometimes, to modify what we had taken for granted. Evidently one danger is that we assimilate whatever we encounter to what we are already familiar with. But that danger can be minimised, if not ever completely eliminated, if we stress the provisionality and revisability of those starting assumptions of ours.

How does that work in practice, and indeed is it over-optimistic to think that we can achieve any such revisions? Some invoke a strong notion of incommensurability and argue that conceptual systems are intelligible only internally; that is, from within the system in question. There are two mistakes to be avoided here. The first is to conclude from a recognition of the contrasts between different sets of concepts that they are strictly mutually unintelligible: on that view <u>no</u> understanding <u>across</u> systems is possible. But the second, converse, mistake is to underestimate the difficulties of achieving any such understanding. In both cases the very idea that concepts <u>form a system</u> may impede progress, for that may mask not just the complexity of the interrelations between concepts and categories but also their open-endedness and even fuzziness. I shall come back to that in a minute.

The present project aims therefore to explore not just some of the varieties of modes of thought and reasoning, but also the limits of mutual intelligibility that are achievable and how that is to be done, including at what cost to the stability of our own initial assumptions. But if that is in effect at this stage just a statement of an article of faith – that some understanding of the other is possible – we have to be clear what the hoped-for understanding is about. On the one hand we must be aware, throughout, of the constraints and limitations of our inquiry, and the limitations include those of the possible use we can make of the findings of other researchers in many related disciplines. On the other hand, our inquiry focuses, among other things, on the very nature of the constraints to which human reasoning in general is subject.

Thus far I have been writing as if reasoning were a matter of the pure exercise of the intelligence, mediated through language. But that clearly will not do. We have first to factor in the pragmatics of the situations in which communication takes place, for reasoning is not solely nor even primarily a matter of the mind's internal dialogue just with itself. Far more often it involves interaction with a real or imagined audience, present or past or even future. Even as we endeavour to work out what we hold to be the case on any important subject, we are probably aware of when those ideas of ours will face the crucial test of others' reactions. Sooner or later we have an audience to persuade and how we set about that task will certainly reflect our views of <u>their</u> likely expectations, including what may seem to us to be their prejudices.

The situation is often far more complex than that. Much communication uses channels that are familiar enough: we use language as carefully as we can to get our points across, aware that what we express in one natural language may be difficult to convey in another. But what about where language altogether fails or is irrelevant, when the knowledge we wish to convey is a matter of practice, of the skill in performing a task, for instance, where precisely what the skill consists in cannot be put into words? Much that is relevant to our understanding of cognition and intelligence escapes an analysis of spoken or written words, existing below the threshold of any such analysis, and even when words do pass as the common coin of communication, there is so much more to what is communicated than is captured by an examination of their bare syntax and semantics.

That is the point at which to introduce a conjecture that has far-reaching repercussions, both for the conduct of this inquiry and for our substantive conclusions concerning the answers to the questions we have posed. I am referring to the unorthodox notion that I have introduced elsewhere, that of semantic stretch. My original aim was to escape from the seemingly all-pervasive dichotomy of the literal and the metaphorical. Its many disadvantages include the difficulty of establishing any clear boundary between the two, the expectation that is created that what the metaphor is a metaphor for should be able to be cashed out in literal terms, and especially the common assumption that the literal should be the norm and that the metaphorical is deviant. Semantic stretch, by contrast, allows that any term may exhibit some stretch – a range of interactive meanings which may all contribute to our understanding of what the term conveys in any given collocation.

True, literality has been the recurrent demand of those who require univocity in order to proceed to a logical analysis of the relationships between well-formed formulae. From that point of view semantic stretch may seem to have a high price to pay, in threatening to undermine any such analysis. On the other hand, in other contexts, where formal logic is not in play, it has the advantage that it can do justice to the complexities and flexibility of most human communication and reasoning. Abandoning the mirage that everything that is worth saying has to or should observe the canons of univocity, it can allow for those complexities. But does this not condemn us to hopeless vagueness and fudge? Not if we see that while every term may have some stretch, that is not to say that that is indefinitely extendable. Terms cannot be made to mean just anything in the manner of Humpty Dumpty, though the range of what they can and do encompass is indeed considerable and liable to be underestimated if we apply the straitjacket of the demand for univocity.

I shall have more to say on this subsequently but for now we may note the implications of this move for my whole project. On the one hand, the terms in which it is to be conducted exhibit semantic stretch. On the other, the recognition of this feature of language constitutes an important substantive conclusion for our understanding of human reasoning.

The problems of assessing both recurrent patterns, and major divergences, within human reasoning are not specific to one domain of scholarly inquiry. Different researchers will tackle different aspects of the question, using different evidence and methods. So I must draw attention to both the limits and the limitations of what shall be attempted here. Let me first acknowledge some notable differences. Palaeontologists will endeavour to plot the changes that marked out *Homo sapiens* from the hominids, where anatomical differences can, up to a point, lead to conjectures about how different species interacted with one another and with their environment. Developmental psychologists can investigate how present-day children acquire the concepts and the skills in reasoning they do, though this field of inquiry suffers from one potential major drawback. This is that the children in question have in the past usually been drawn from particular groups in industrialised societies. That may be less so nowadays, but when it continues to be the case, the extent to which the results suggested can be generalised can be highly problematic. The examination of the diversity of human performance is rather the purview of ethnography, though here too the question of the generalisability of conclusions from any one society to the human condition as a whole must be confronted. Indeed there is not just that question, but, as we have already noted, the prior one of how far mutual intelligibility is possible.[1] Of course, if there is no desire to understand the Other, there is no more to be said. I shall be more concerned with the less extreme case, where the obstacles to mutual understanding are thought to stem from the differences in beliefs and practices themselves. This is where an opportunity for progress presents itself, if we can lay the bogey of radical incommensurability.

[1] I am not presupposing that we can lay down strict criteria for what counts as 'mutual intelligibility', only that we have some, however fallible, grasp of what it is to understand others and to be understood.

The particular evidence I seek to make the most of, in these studies, relates to ancient societies. Of course this poses its own severe set of problems, notably both the bias and the lacunae in the sources available to us. We cannot interview our subjects. The overwhelming majority of our evidence comes from the writings that happened to survive. We have no reason to believe that these are a representative sample of what was actually produced, for most of what we have stems from members of the literate elite. True, we can supplement our written sources with the material remains, particularly helpful for the study of certain facets of ancient societies, the available technology, for example, and their social arrangements. But for the beliefs and practices of most members of ancient societies we rely on what we can gather from those elite writings and we must accordingly allow for their preconceptions and *parti pris*.

Yet even though our evidence suffers from such systemic weaknesses, it does have an advantage over much ethnography in one respect, and that is that we can more readily trace changes that occurred across time. Moreover, if we seek to chart similarities and differences as between ancient and modern societies, the very fact that the latter inherited so much from the former can prove to be an advantage, for we can study just what changed and what remained constant in the complex processes involved. A recurrent topic of concern will be in what precise respects our common modernist assumptions consciously or unconsciously reflect those of our predecessors. It is obvious that what we think of as Western preoccupations owed much to the legacy of Graeco-Roman antiquity (even when the Moderns chose to represent themselves as radically different from the Ancients). But just to what extent those preoccupations figured elsewhere in the world and at different periods is one of the key issues with which we must come to terms.

Now first, a careful examination of the Graeco-Roman legacy itself reveals just how complex that was and how contentious – among the ancient Greeks themselves. They certainly had a lot to say about reason, though there are important shifts in the understandings of the key terms and in the views expressed on the substantive problems.[2] Thus initially, in Homer, the map of the cognitive faculties does not include one that tallies exactly with what we mean by 'reason', and for Homer what survives death is an insubstantial wraith, not (as later in Plato) an immortal soul ontologically contrasted with the body.[3] Yet from the beginnings of Greek

---

[2] The volume edited by Frede and Striker 1996 provides a notable collection of studies of that variety.

[3] In a vast literature on the pre-philosophical Greek background, I may single out Onians 1951 and Snell 1953 as particularly influential, especially the latter's thesis (later much criticised by Padel 1992, among others) that the mind was a Greek discovery.

speculative philosophy such issues as the relation between reason and perception, and reason and desire, come to be debated, as do questions to do
with the limits of the powers of reason and others concerning whether other
creatures besides humans have reason and whether all humans do to an
equal degree. Aristotle, who knew a lot about animals' behaviour and skills,
denied they have reason, though some of them have intelligence, *phronēsis*,
even if, in their case, that does not depend on a moral faculty. Notoriously he allots only a limited capacity for rational thought to women and
to slaves, and children have none until they become responsible adults.[4] A
final complication is that, for Aristotle and several other Greek thinkers,
humans share reason in the sense of the theoretical faculty with God.

If we want to clarify what faculties, concerns and practices are indeed
common to most humans, then we need to examine both ancient and
modern societies that were not influenced by that Graeco-Roman legacy.
Ancient China in this respect provides an especially useful foil to ancient
Greece. The ancient Chinese were less preoccupied with epistemological
issues, the tendency to support first-order substantive claims by appeal to
second-order arguments about the sources of understanding. In the *scala
naturae* that we find in the third-century BCE writer Xunzi, what marks
out humans from the other animals is not reason (as in Aristotle) but rather
morality.[5] The Chinese sage does not exhibit his pre-eminence by engaging
in Aristotelian intellectual reasoning, but by his wisdom. Chinese investigations into the world around them did not make use of an overarching
concept of nature, nor postulate an ontological gulf between Seeming and
Being. They certainly reflected on language and on methods of persuasion and argument, but without deploying the contrast between the literal
and the metaphorical. Even that bare statement of differences identifies
the challenge we face. Can we make sense of those divergent viewpoints,
both Greek and Chinese? What consequences do the Chinese concepts and
practices have for our evaluation of the Greek legacy?

The subjects I tackle in the studies that follow are just a few of those that
can be used to scrutinise just some of the common fundamental assumptions made in our attempts to understand one another and the world
around us. But they seem to me to offer notable opportunities both for
the detailed comparisons and contrasts between Ancients and Moderns I
have just alluded to, and for reflections on the commonalities and cross-
cultural divergences in human reasoning more generally.

---

[4] See Sorabji 1993, Osborne 2007, Lloyd 2012a.   [5] See Lloyd 2012a: 14–15 on *Xunzi* 9: 16a.

Is rationality a well-defined human universal, such that ideas and behaviour can everywhere be judged by a single set of criteria or standards? In that case the analogy would be with biologically determined diseases, where biomedical science offers descriptions of distinct syndromes and symptoms and can often identify specific causes. At the opposite extreme is the view that rational and irrational are simply cultural constructs, varying across populations as well as individuals. There the (imperfect) analogy would be with the concept of illness insofar as that depends on subjective judgements. The position I shall argue for endeavours to avoid the weaknesses of both those options. The universalist thesis tends to underestimate the multiplicity of criteria to which we can and should appeal in assessing sound arguments and practices. On the relativist side, conversely, we need to admit the strength of the universalist claim that all humans everywhere have always argued, inferred, reasoned, persuaded, even though the ways they do so and the successes they achieve vary. The present studies therefore aim to explore the heterogeneity of what can validly be called rational and to caution against a still-common exclusive use of that concept. The rational is what we have to rely on, for sure, but we must be aware of how much eludes its confident grasp and how dangerous may be some of its pretensions to deliver certainty.

We must recognise that the threats to mutual understanding and tolerance that we currently face stretch far beyond what a merely abstract analysis can achieve. I shall return to that issue in my concluding chapter. Nevertheless my aim throughout is to make some small contribution to our self-awareness, principally by way of an examination of what may be considered the master binary of rationality and the irrational. My first study undertakes a preliminary critical scrutiny of that dichotomy, which will remain present in the background in each of the subsequent chapters before re-emerging as the central theme of my concluding discussion of its ambivalences.

CHAPTER 2

Rationality Reviewed

Rationality has meant many different things to different people and a little history may serve to identify some of the many confusions it may generate. In the 1970s and 1980s there was a flurry of debate in which it was often assumed that the antonym of rationality is relativism. That was one of the themes or preoccupations of the collection of essays edited by Bryan Wilson under the title *Rationality* in 1970. Then a second collection, edited by Hollis and Lukes in 1982, took *Rationality and Relativism* as its title (cf. Jarvie 1983). To quote the blurb of that book,

> Are there any universal forms of reasoning, of understanding, or is every-thing relative? Can other cultures, other languages, other scientific frame-works only be understood from within, discussed only in their own terms? Should we – indeed can we – distinguish between beliefs which are rational and those which, in various ways, are not? If so, does that affect the kind of explanation to be sought?

That last question was an allusion to the so-called strong programme of the Edinburgh school, much discussed in that volume,[1] according to which it is not just erroneous beliefs that should be the subject of inquiry, but also correct ones.

That volume marked a particular moment when various brands of ratio-nality were thought to need defence in the face of certain movements in sociology and anthropology. But of course the debate did not start there. Weber (1948) had already attempted one clarification by insisting on the contrast between various <u>modes</u> of rationality, notably means–ends rationality (*Zweckrationalität*) and value-oriented *Wertrationalität*.[2] That allows us to class as 'rational' certain rule-following procedures or activities

---

[1] It contained an article by Barnes and Bloor (1982), although the majority of the contributors disagreed with them.

[2] The criteria that are relevant to assessing values had, of course, much earlier been distinguished from those appropriate to evaluating facts, notably by Hume.

whether or not we think the rules themselves are well founded. Astrology is certainly rational in the sense that the practitioners have to apply certain rules. But the question whether they have done so consistently is independent of the issue whether those rules are well grounded. The problem, then, is <u>who</u> is to assess whether they are: I shall need to revert to that repeatedly.

Complicating the issue further, Simon Blackburn's *Oxford Dictionary of Philosophy* has this to say on 'Rationality' (Blackburn 2008: 307):

> Pieces of behaviour, beliefs, arguments, policies, and other exercises of the human mind may all be described as rational. To accept something as rational is to accept it as making sense, as appropriate, or required, or in accordance with some acknowledged goal, such as aiming at truth or aiming at the good.

Blackburn then goes on to distinguish different positions taken on whether rationality is what marks out humans from other animals, on whether the exercise of reason is part of the highest good for humans ('Plato and Aristotle'), and on whether it secures freedom of decision or is simply a slave of the passions (Kant and Hegel versus Hume).

Even allowing for the broad brush that has to be used in philosophical dictionaries, we can see the tension between the normative and the would-be descriptive. If it is what 'makes sense' or is 'appropriate', we have to ask, to whom? Who is to be the judge (cf. Davidson 2004: ch. 3)?[3] If it is a universal human faculty, how does that square with our sense that quite a lot of the time it is switched off, and quite a lot of the time it misfires – though it is important to keep in mind this distinction between the faculty and the use; that is, between capacity and performance. Differences in the modes of reasoning cultivated do not entitle us to conclude that some humans have, but others lack, any capacity for rational thought at all, even though, as we have seen, that was the route that Aristotle took.

Plenty of clever people have tackled the problems before me, but it is alarming how much of what has been proposed now seems like special pleading, aimed at bolstering some antecedent conviction, for example that humans <u>must</u> be different from other animals, or again that humans <u>must</u> all have the same cognitive abilities – or again the opposites of those

---

[3] The difficulty of finding a judge who is not already *parti pris* is a trope in ancient Chinese sources, as for example in *Zhuangzi* ch. 2: 84–90 (I shall be considering this text in some detail in ch. 3). The point is generalised to support a radical sceptical argument to undermine any claim to establish a criterion of truth, whether in reason or perception, in the second-century CE Greek author Sextus Empiricus (*Outlines of Pyrrhonism* 2: 14–79).

convictions, that humans <u>cannot</u> be different from other animals or that it is obvious that we do <u>not</u> all have the same cognitive abilities.[4]

But are we in any position to do any better? How can we release ourselves from <u>our</u> antecedent convictions; that is, our prejudices? Obviously a *tu quoque* demand for reflexivity is appropriate. What prior assumptions are we bringing to the task? How does our own formation or upbringing affect the way we pose the questions, let alone the conclusions we would like to come out sound? The risks of prejudice are always there and we can never be sure we have got to the bottom of all our assumptions. Yet we can aim to do as conscientious a job as possible – and then we just have to get on with it.

But we can say at least that in 2017 the possibility of bringing to bear the recent findings of new areas of inquiry exists, even though what conclusions that new work suggests is still up for grabs. Let me pass under review very briefly four such areas, palaeontology, ethology, developmental psychology and anthropology. As I say, what precisely we should make of these developments is not always clear – and that is true for those in the forefront of these fields, not just for outsiders such as myself. But I believe that the cumulative effect is to make it more difficult to sustain uniqueness claims, whether (even) for humans as unique among the animals, or for certain groups as unique among humans. That may leave as the default option that a capacity for reason is universal, though how it is used differs. Then the question becomes: how does that work out in practice? The workings or the use of that supposed universal faculty have still to be investigated: that is where the difficulties arise, and where we should concentrate our efforts to clarify the issues.

So I turn first to palaeontology, a field of research that certainly attempts to pin down what gave humans an evolutionary advantage over other animals, including over our now no longer extant nearest relatives, the hominids. That might be a matter of certain physical characteristics such as are involved in the greater capacity to vocalisation and so to communication, or of social ones. Here Humphrey (1976), Tooby and Cosmides (1989, 1992) and Mercier and Sperber (2011, 2017) are among the key players. At the same time some cognitive scientists, such as Kahneman and Tversky,[5] have suggested that a number of characteristic modes of error in

---

[4] I discussed the commonalities and divergences in human cognitive capacities in Lloyd 2007a, and some of the many various positions that have been adopted on the relation between humans and other animals in Lloyd 2012a: ch. 1.

[5] See, for example, Tversky and Kahneman 1982; Evans 1989; Nickerson 1998; Mercier and Sperber 2011, 2017.

reasoning (such as the confirmation bias)[6] go back to the cognitive capacities laid down already in the Pleistocene. Yet if humans certainly engaged
and engage in 'fast and frugal' reasoning (Gigerenzer and Goldstein 1996,
Kahneman 2011), we are not alone. Other animals also needed and need to
do so in order to survive. Hesitation over the identification of a predator
or of a prey is not a recipe for success for any living creature.

The thrust of these palaeontological arguments is first to underline what
we share with other animals. Second, if there are points at which humans
are indeed distinctive, it is humans as a whole who are such, not some
privileged group of us. Thus our basic vocal apparatus is species-wide. True,
the manners in which we socialise are very diverse, but the fact that we
socialise somehow is common, as Aristotle recognised when he defined a
human being as naturally (*phusei*) a social animal, a *politikon zōon*, ideally
one that lives in a city-state, *polis*, even though he knew full well that the
majority of humans did not. Whatever else may be contentious in that
view, it draws attention to the point that to survive, humans depend on
other humans.

Ethology, the study of animal behaviour, overlaps at points, as those
remarks already indicate, with palaeontology. Certainly ethologists too are
concerned with what marks out humans from other animals. Yet many of
the favourite criteria confidently invoked for that purpose have tended to
be eroded, even though differences in degree continue to be recognised.
Humans are clearly not the only tool users, nor are we the only creatures
who communicate complex messages to one another (including about how
to use those tools) by signs and sounds.[7] Nor, as Aristotle already also
insisted, are we the only social animals. Operating in groups can evidently
carry an evolutionary advantage, though it also presents its problems. But
to obviate some of those, we are not the only animals to have devised
cheater-detection mechanisms and ways of limiting the damage caused
by freeloaders (e.g. Cosmides and Tooby 1992; Dunbar 1999). There is a
constant arms race, in fact, between those who are intent on beating the
system – one that ensures that we all take our fair share of our joint respon-
sibilities – and those who hope the system is robust enough to work.

---

[6] The 'confirmation bias' refers to a widely attested tendency: we are far better at finding support for
what we antecedently assume than at searching for and evaluating counterevidence.

[7] Among the best-attested examples of the transmission and learning of tool use is among chimpanzees,
where there is now a considerable literature; see Boesch and Boesch 1984; McGrew 1992; Boesch 1996;
Humle and Matsuzawa 2002. The classic study of the range of vocal communication among birds is
that of Catchpole and Slater 2008, while there are reviews of research on vervet communication in
Seyfarth and Cheney 1982 and Cheney and Seyfarth 1990. Cf. Lloyd 2012a: 9–10.

The upshot of much of this work, too, is to narrow the gap between humans and other creatures. It is just as well to remind ourselves that we as humans are just as likely to rely on hunches – that is, non-deductive inference – as on strict logic. Formal logic is fine for the logic classroom where there are plenty of well-formed formulae or wffs around. But for practical purposes what we need is effective informal logic, maybe even with a touch of *mētis*, cunning intelligence, thrown in. We should recall that, where *mētis* is concerned, the Greeks recognised plenty of paradigmatic examples from the animal kingdom: the octopus, the fox, the spider.[8]

Next there are studies in child development where, however (as with much other psychological research), I have certain qualms about some aspects of the methodology. Ever since Piaget (1929, 1930, 1959) the children whose developing understanding of the external world has been investigated have been drawn from a particular, generally quite narrow, range of backgrounds. According to a recent, iconoclastic, article by Henrich, Heine and Norenzayan (2010), bias still contaminates much psychological research insofar as the subjects examined are the 'weirdest' people in the world, Western, Educated, Industrialised, Rich and Democratic – outliers, not typical of humanity as a whole. When that is the case, that does not invalidate the results for the population concerned, but it does undermine their generalisability. In recent years, sustained studies of non-Weird subjects have certainly been on the increase, but the Weird ones continue to dominate the field.

However, the types of results that have traditionally been claimed in psychology relate to the transitions, whether in individuals or in whole groups, from a naive or a folk understanding of certain topics to a more 'advanced', even 'scientific', one. Naive physics (for example) does not recognise the principle of conservation: when a quantity of water is poured from a wide jug into a narrower one and reaches a higher level, this is not because the amount of water has increased. Naive psychology imputes agency to all kinds of objects, where adult psychology knows better (or is supposed to). In the case of folk or naive biology, however, which may be ascribed not just to children growing up but to whole communities, the anthropologist Scott Atran and his associates have made a case that it is rarely superseded by scientific taxonomy. Rather it underpins a universal human apprehension of similarities and differences in the plant and animal kingdoms.[9] Of course,

---

[8] The classic study of Greek *mētis* is Detienne and Vernant 1978. I reviewed some of the examples that Aristotle gives of animal intelligence in Lloyd 2013.

[9] See, for example Atran 1990, 1998; Medin and Atran 1999; Atran, Medin and Ross 2004. Cf. Lloyd 2007a: ch. 3.

in a looser or more mundane usage of 'psychology' no one is going to deny that human character traits differ within any given group, as well as across different ones. There is nothing surprising in the former: it is only if we credit old-fashioned ideas that stereotype national characters that the latter militates against commonalities across humankind; but with one exception that I shall come back to (Nisbett), such ideas rest on no more than anecdotal evidence at best, and usually just reflect more or less open racial prejudice. In general, work in psychology often testifies to a desire to find major differences between individuals and within human populations, but the claims made often seem to outrun the concrete evidence for them.

That has already taken me into my fourth subject area, social anthropology, often represented as the greatest threat to human universality and the bastion of relativism. I shall proceed with due caution to assess where, if anywhere, there are grounds for surprise, let alone for scandal and the possible verdict of irrationality. We can start from the absolutely banal observation that customs differ. You wear white dresses at funerals, we at marriages. You do not cut your facial hair, we do. You practise polyandry and or polygamy, we are monogamous. From there we approach ethically more sensitive issues. You do not kill and eat living creatures, we do. You do not consider your enemies to be humans, for us they are.

The variety of mores was a topos in ancient Mesopotamia, in ancient Greece and Rome, and at the other end of the Eurasian land mass in China. Any society that has any knowledge of other groups is bound to recognise that they are different from themselves, for they would not be 'other' unless they were in some way different. That was almost invariably accompanied by the thought that 'our' ways (whatever they were) are superior to 'theirs', but it was accepted that 'they' had their traditions just as much as 'we' did. The variety was understood. The problems arose first where morality is concerned, and second where it was thought that some sets of beliefs or practices were foolish or even deluded, which is where especially the topic of irrationality is implicated.

One reaction to the realisation of the great diversity of moral beliefs was to set out on a hunt for universal moral principles. The incest taboo, so it was thought, was the best candidate for a universally accepted social rule – except that the trouble was that what counted as such was not without its equivocations. Brother–sister royal marriages were sacred, not prohibited.[10] Then various formulations of what has been dubbed the Golden Rule are

[10] The disputed question of the biological and sociological factors in play in various types of avoidance was much discussed in the wake of Lévi-Strauss 1969 (originally 1949). For a recent survey of ancient Egyptian practices, see Scheidel 2004.

found in many ancient societies, China, India, Egypt, Greece and Israel. The negative version says 'do not unto others as you would not have them do to you', but there is also a positive form, namely 'do unto others as you would have them do unto you'. This is a principle that gathers some empirical support from the study of children's behaviour in the playground where such research has been undertaken (though, as noted, this has mostly been on Weird children).[11] Yet Universal Declarations of Human Rights have been honoured more in the breach than in the observance. Besides, with the exception of cases where some inconsistency can be detected,[12] to label those with other moral principles than our own as <u>irrational</u> is usually no more than another way of registering our disagreement and disapproval.

The 1980s debate spent a lot of time worrying not just about cross-cultural bases of morality, but also about what were dubbed apparently irrational beliefs or practices. The Nuer were reported as believing that twins are birds (Evans-Pritchard 1956), the Dorze that the leopard is a Christian animal (Sperber 1985), the Azande did not take important decisions without consulting the poison oracle, and so on and so on (Evans-Pritchard 1937). As I remarked before, some concluded that such items could only be understood <u>within</u> the system of beliefs in question, the idea being that these systems were incommensurable with one another, taken to mean that there was no common criterion by which they could be judged.

Yet as soon as one looked beyond categorical assertions of mutual unintelligibility to what else was reported of the societies in question, the idea that simply nothing could be understood by outsiders seemed increasingly bizarre. After all, the contexts in which the Azande poison oracle was invoked could be itemised and the concerns of the practitioners to secure a decision on a matter of importance in a way that would command common acceptance were clearly understandable. True, an adequate understanding of those contexts and concerns was always hard to come by, for the ethnographers themselves, let alone for armchair critics such as the philosophers and sociologists who made up the majority of the participants in the 1980s debate (and of course I have to include myself as such an armchair observer). Nor were the parallels with more widely accepted beliefs and practices in our own 'advanced' society lost on everyone. For the Christian God is Three and He is One. In the Mass the wafer becomes the flesh of Christ and the wine his blood. (The parallelism with what is reported

---

[11] Gary Matthews's work with children as they puzzle over moral, among other philosophical, questions also lends some support to the principle (Matthews 1984, 1994).

[12] There is good ancient Chinese evidence of an awareness of the problems posed by inconsistency: see Lloyd 2014: 127; and cf. below, ch. 5, p. 69.

from Amazonian societies is startling: I am thinking of those reports that have it that when the jaguar drinks the blood of the prey, for the jaguar that is not blood but manioc beer).[13] The extra bit that some Christian apologists explicitly added was that in judging the mysteries and sacraments of the true religion, reason was no good: you have to rely on faith, *pistis*. As Tertullian was to put it in the context of belief in the Resurrection, 'Having been buried, He rose again. This is certain because it is impossible' (*Certum est quia impossibile*).[14]

Puzzling, counterintuitive, mystificatory even, statements and items of behaviour can be found in any society and pose challenges of interpretation, where one response may be that we have to suspend some of our own usual assumptions or otherwise to work harder to grasp what is going on, but where our final reaction may be that we are indeed faced with a mystery, if not a deliberate mystification. Note that this differs in one respect from Davidson's principle of charity in interpretation (Davidson 2001); that is, the recommendation that to understand some alien conceptual scheme we should work to make it make sense – so far as possible – in our terms. The difference is that in the view I favour we have to emphasise that 'our' terms will have to be revised as we proceed in our task. But note also that success is in no way guaranteed. At the end of the day we may well have to admit that we do not understand.

That last is an especially important point to bear in mind with regard to more recent anthropological discussion which makes the 1980s examples seem almost trivial by comparison. We have Viveiros de Castro (1998) and Descola (2013) especially to thank for opening up the problems and increasing their scope and relevance dramatically. Here with Viveiros de Castro's perspectivism and Descola's fourfold ontologies we are dealing not with isolated items of belief or practice, but with radically divergent worlds or worldings, as Descola puts it – ways of being in a world.

Although the importance of these ideas has been recognised well beyond the specialist circles of social anthropologists, a brief digression is necessary to outline the points relevant to my discussion here. Quite how 'ontological' Descola's ontologies are is debatable: they do not come supported with batteries of indigenous philosophical arguments in the manner of a Kant, a Plato or a Parmenides (Severi 2013). But the term 'ontology' is certainly justified, as an observer's category, in that it focuses on the quite distinctive perceptions of interiority (the self) and physicality (the body: what

---

[13] See especially Viveiros de Castro 1998; Vilaça 2010; Descola 2013. Cf. Lloyd 2012a: 18–19, 107–9.
[14] Tertullian, *On the Flesh of Christ*: ch. 5. He had just said, 'The Son of God is dead: this is to be believed, because it is absurd' (*credibile est, quia ineptum est*).

things are made of) that are in play. Descola's four are distinguished according to whether they assume continuities or discontinuities on either axis. Thus what he calls 'naturalism', the default ontology of Western modernity, assumes discontinuities between humans and other beings in interiority (humans alone have culture) but continuities in physicality (we are all made of the same stuff). 'Animism', as he redefines that, assumes the reverse, a continuity in interiority (not only humans but also other animals have culture) but discontinuity in physicality (what separates things is their bodies, their natures: it is because the jaguar has the body it does that it behaves in the way it does). Totemism (again redefined) adopts continuities on both axes, and 'analogism', his fourth ontology, discontinuities on both, though connecting the items thus distinguished precisely by analogies. One of the principal pay-offs of the whole schema comes when Descola is able to correlate the particular ontologies in question with different modes of exchange, including, for example, sacrifice (not common in totemic or animist societies, but frequent in analogistic ones) (Descola 2013: 228).

Viveiros de Castro has reservations about that schema but in one important regard joins forces with Descola. He too sets in opposition to the usual Western assumption of mononaturalism plus multiculturalism a view that he finds widespread across many peoples of the world, where it is culture that is common, nature diverse; monoculturalism, in other words, plus multinaturalism (Viveiros de Castro 1998: 470–1). Again the key point is the belief that other creatures besides humans have cultures. What makes different creatures different is the bodies they possess. This, he insists, is not (just) a different world view, but a different world, underlining the incommensurabilities, and so the challenges to understanding involved.

Now we must be clear from the outset that the members of the groups whom Descola labels animist and whom Viveiros de Castro uses to illustrate perspectivism manifest the highest forms of intelligence in dealing with the problems of everyday life. To learn how to make efficient, dead-straight, blowpipes of the right, even, bore and length, and to tip the darts used with the right dose of the poison, curare, that has to be extracted and prepared from the relevant plants with the utmost care, are just two examples I pick up from Descola's earlier book (Descola 1996). Where Westerners, whether as individuals or in groups, would not survive long, the Achuar got on fine for centuries. I put that in the past tense since with 'contact' so much has changed. Initially, for instance, their frequent intergroup battles became increasingly lethal once they exchanged their bows and arrows and blowpipes for the firearms they obtained from Western traders and missionaries. But if they are now armed with guns, they have also been 'pacified'.

But when we hear (Descola 1996: ch. 6, ch. 8) that Achuar women sing to the plants in their gardens and that Achuar men use encoded language so that the monkeys they hunt should not suspect that they will be attacked, the reaction that that is not necessary and is in fact irrational is where we are liable, among other things, to underestimate the reach of the total cosmology they sign up to. For the Achuar, animals and even some plants resemble humans in that they exhibit social relations, at least patterns of behaviour such as attitudes of friendship and co-operation or of hostility. That is not a view we generally share. But instead of dismissing theirs as foolish and irrational, we might do better to reflect on what we might ourselves learn from treating other living beings as closer to us and more like us than we normally assume. As for beliefs that to ensure success in a hunt it is not a bad idea to carry out some ritual that you may have used in the past, I am reminded of a colleague of mine at Cambridge who never went fishing without a favourite pebble in his pocket.

Many of the personal or socially sanctioned rituals we and they engage in should be judged not by the canons of efficacy (do they in fact work, causally producing as their effect some desired result) but rather by the criteria of felicity (Tambiah 1973: 220 ff.; cf. Tambiah 1990: ch. 1). The question which it is proper to ask is: is it the appropriate kind of behaviour? We may recall Blackburn's invocation of appropriateness in his analysis of 'rationality', and where the stronger term 'felicity' is used, that may be to suggest the positive contribution that is being made to well-being or happiness. The example I have used before is showering the bride and groom with confetti at a wedding. That is not now generally believed actually to ensure their fertility – which may have been the rationalising justification offered at one time – but it is an action performed because it is the done thing (or was) at Christian weddings. Without the confetti, the wedding would not, somehow, be a proper one. The rationale of what might be thought a bit of 'magic' would then be not that 'it works' but that it is the socially sanctioned way of doing things, contributing to group solidarity, and accordingly in that respect perfectly 'rational'.

However, the question does not just go away: we cannot be content with saying that it is the pressures of social solidarity that account for much otherwise irrational-seeming belief and behaviour, even though that may be the case in many instances. For the follow-up question is how those beliefs and behaviour got to be socially sanctioned in the first place. Were they, we can ask, at any point subject to scrutiny or doubt? Who was in a position to question or challenge them? Within what limits was dissent allowed?

It is obvious that we are thus taken into an analysis of the social structures and interrelations of the group or society in question, a topic that leads inevitably into further questions of the differences that literacy and social complexity generally may introduce, though, as I shall argue in chapter 5, they are not to be answered in terms of yet another binary, the Domesticated versus the Savage Mind. However, if we are looking for instances of the different ways in which the faculty of reasoning may be used, then one promising area of investigation is the degree and modes of toleration of dissent – and how they are expressed – that are found. These are certainly difficult questions to answer with the available ethnographic evidence, but we shall see that where ancient societies are concerned, we can sometimes trace the changing dynamics of the possibilities of scepticism and disagreement.

I have hardly scratched the surface where the possible relevance of ethnographic fieldwork is concerned. But I have yet to tackle directly one final area where the triumphs of rationality are especially trumpeted, namely with the advent of a proper scientific way of deciding questions. Quite how that is to be defined and when it is to be dated are controversial. I have gone on record (Lloyd 2000) as dismissing the idea that 'science' itself can be said to have had an origin, or even several, for I am swayed by the argument that the principal methods that science relies on go back to humans' very first attempts to understand and control the world around them. Systematic observation is a development of common-or-garden observation. Experiment is a more explicit and controlled application of much earlier trial-and-error methods – and so on. To be sure, other aspects of scientific practice, and notably several of the 'styles' that Hacking (1992, 2009, 2012) has identified, do have datable historical origins, indeed often quite recent ones. Quantitative notions of probability, for instance, do not antedate the sixteenth century, computer modelling is even more recent and 'laboratory life' presupposes the modern institution of laboratories. But while the tools of investigation have developed, not to have those tools is no sign of irrationality. Again developments in systematicity and self-conscious explicitness did undoubtedly occur, and not just in the so-called Scientific Revolution. Yet that does not mean that the faculty, reason, itself has changed, only that the instruments it can draw on have.

I would be cautious, therefore, in answering the question of how far those developments represented an increase in rationality and the diminution of the grip of the irrational. Of course science has secured many robust results and solutions to problems that otherwise remained intensely baffling. Yet science's reach has its limits and it may be argued that our sense of what we do not as yet understand grows as fast as our grasp of what we do. Besides, scientists are certainly not immune to making mistakes, individual ones and ones involving complexes of ideas and theories. They do their best to avoid those at work, but what about their private lives: do they never curse their cars when they fail to start? That is a cheap point to make, but it will more readily be agreed that sometimes peer-group pressure in the lab has been known to cloud the judgement of individuals and even of the group as a whole.

More importantly, science does not tell us all we need to know in such areas as psychology, let alone in morality. But the advances that have been made can be recognised as such without leading to any global conclusion to the effect that there is some Great Divide separating those who have access to science from those in other times or places who do not. By that I mean that access to science does not guarantee rationality in any of the senses that I have identified, any more than not having such access precludes it.

It is particularly important, perhaps, to unmask the implicit imperialism that went with the idea that science is a peculiarly Western phenomenon. Here I must come back to Nisbett, whose book (2003) was subtitled *How Asians and Westerners Think Differently . . . and Why*. This cites experimental evidence that he claims shows that there are indeed systematic differences in 'how people think', including the individualism of Westerners and the greater sense of social solidarity among Asiatics (a thesis also promulgated by Markus and Kitayama 1991, among others). The first problem here relates to the categories he operates with. 'Asiatics' includes not just Chinese on the mainland and on Taiwan, but also Chinese of the diaspora, including citizens of the United States, as well as Japanese and Koreans, two peoples who normally consider the differences between themselves and the Chinese to be greater than the similarities. As for 'Westerners', these include 'European Americans, blacks and whites and Hispanics', as well as ancient Greeks.

The differences that emerge from his researches are more economically explained by differences in the values entertained by the people investigated, rather than by differences in the way they reason. So while, obviously, there are differences in the way the faculty is used as between different individuals and different groups, there are no grounds here for asserting that the faculty itself differs as such. As I said, the diagnosis of irrationality is often just a particularly emotive way of expressing disagreement or disapproval. When the problem is, as in Blackburn, what 'makes sense' or 'is appropriate or required', we may always ask who is to judge that and on what grounds. Sometimes, to be sure, those grounds withstand our best scrutiny: but obviously that is not always the case.

So it is time to take stock. I have made it clear that I have quite a few reservations about just how useful the notion of the irrational is (and so, conversely, also of the rational), though I can see that it is worth following up the consequences and biases of certain favoured modes of reasoning, as indeed I have been doing for analogy now for several years. When the source or justification of the diagnosis of irrationality is inconsistency, that may serve as a useful tool of analysis, though even here it may be worth considering under what conditions seemingly inconsistent statements or beliefs may be reconciled (charity again).

But when 'irrational' is the term used to label a whole cosmology – either a world view, or a way of being in a world, or even a world or ontology itself – we need to be especially wary. A whole cosmology is not to be expressed in a well-formed formula, nor even in a series of them. Quite what commitments are being made to how things are or how one should behave requires patient interpretation. I shall be attempting some such explorations in the chapters that follow. To deliver a verdict of foolishness or irrationality is to forgo the opportunity to learn, to see things from a new perspective, even if, after we have done our best at learning, we choose not to agree (as may often be the case). There are fools in every society, mistakes are made by even the most intelligent people and as I noted there are some recurrent errors in reasoning that may be deeply engrained as a legacy from our evolutionary past. It is always difficult to understand one another, even those with whom one shares a single natural language and a similar background. This is so much the more difficult across different languages, let alone across ontologies. Yet some understanding, I would say, is always possible,[15] and can be increased if one works at it in the belief that it *is* possible, aware that that opportunity is liable to be foreclosed when irrationality is diagnosed.

So how useful is the focus on 'rationality' and what results can we hope for or expect? Given the indeterminacy, not to say confusion, that surrounds the concept, the dangers of circularity are obvious, by which I mean that we shall simply get out whatever we have put into the definition we opt

---

[15] In chapter 6 I shall come back to the difficult case of what is being communicated in reports of mystical experience. The content of that experience may well be intensely personal and subjective and beyond the reach of anyone else. But the outsider gathers this much, that for the mystic this was an altogether unusual event, where mundane descriptions fail even though they are the basis of the only accounts possible.

for. If we go down the universalising route, to make rationality definitive of what it is to be a human being (as so many ancient Greeks did), then the problem is to account for the different patterns of behaviour we find, in the practices of reasoning, in the different skills to which they are applied, and in their degree of explicit self-consciousness. If, alternatively, we go down the relativising route, the converse problem we face is to account for how, as the social animals we are, we all share at least the capacity to use our wits to survive.

Either way, we have a double agenda, to do justice both to the commonalities and to the divergences we encounter. To get clearer about the first is (among other things) a matter of paying attention to the obvious fact that humans everywhere argue, persuade, infer – well or badly, under the influence of unexamined assumptions or even of examined ones. To get clearer about the second we need all the resources of anthropology, psychology, cognitive science, ancient and not so ancient history, while being wary of Grand Theories that diagnose massive breaks or discontinuities: we should be wary of those obviously for the simple reason that they tend to ignore what we all have in common. If there have, indeed, been shifts and changes, these are often a matter of greater self-consciousness, not unconnected, in many cases, with social, political and institutional factors, sometimes with religious or cosmological ones, often reflecting shifts in values. But these are shifts that should not be overdramatised as Grand Divisions in the matter of rationality itself.

It is not a question of choosing between psychic unity and psychic diversity, for I would say (indeed I have gone on record as saying (Lloyd 2007a)) that we need both. But that shifts the agenda to the question of how the two combine, what the unity consists in, how far it stretches and again where the diversities lie and how we account for them. There is still plenty of work to be done, though not in the spirit of advocating one or the other side of the potentially misleading binary. As for rationality and irrationality, despite my sceptical views about their positive usefulness, they are still, I would say, important topics of critical inquiry, with the emphasis on the critical and the focus on the need to unmask the covert agenda they all too often conceal. I shall be considering a variety of examples where that is the case in the studies that follow.

CHAPTER 3

Cosmology without Nature

Cosmology, by which I mean the understanding of the cosmos or the universe as a whole, provides a major field in which it has often been assumed that we can be confident both of what there is to be investigated (reality, as delivered by physics) and of the proper, rational, way of investigating it (through 'science', as opposed to, say, mere speculation or guesswork, let alone superstition or magic). Not to entertain the correct ideas on the subject in question, and again a failure to adopt the right methods, can sometimes be labelled not just mistaken, but irrational. This is in the sense we noted with regard to astrology, which may be rational insofar as it is governed by rules, but is generally dismissed as irrational on the basis that its fundamental assumptions are not well grounded and that its methods are flawed.

Yet both components of the universalist claim that underpins the confidence I have just mentioned are open to challenge. Neither what the cosmos comprises, nor how to deliver robust results in investigating whatever that is, can be said to be unproblematic. So to test the strengths both of the universalist claim and of its relativising rivals we can undertake an examination of the historical development of thought on these issues in ancient societies. Greece and China both provide rich sources of information where it is immediately apparent that in each, divergent views were proposed on the account to be aimed at. As we shall see, many Greeks (not all) saw 'nature', *phusis*, as the target, and offered sophisticated theories about how to go about inquiring into it. Chinese thinkers, by contrast, exemplify the possibility of doing cosmology without any such notion. Yet contrary to the expectation that some positivists might hold, we shall see that it can be argued that in certain respects a cosmology without nature has the edge over one that focuses on that concept. Chinese reflections on the understanding that can be achieved, on the status of human assertions about what is, and on the constitution of physical objects, all provide lessons that are worth pondering, even if in several respects they tend to dislodge some of our own regular preconceptions.

This sets the agenda for this chapter. My first task is to review the major contributions of Greek and Chinese thinkers in all their diversity, where I shall focus first on what I call the Greek invention of nature. Originally, my claim is, the Greeks themselves had no such explicit concept, and no more did any other ancient civilisation. That is not a point I can substantiate across the board here except in the case of China, but confirmation with regard to Mesopotamia at least comes from a recent study significantly entitled *Before Nature* (Rochberg 2016) which undertakes a detailed analysis of Mesopotamian science, particularly the study of the heavens, before such a concept was available.

Nature in Greece was the rubric philosophers and others came to use to mark out what we call natural phenomena and thereby identify a domain of investigation where natural causes could be assigned to events that had previously often (though not always) been thought of by the Greeks themselves as subject to divine intervention. The philosophers in question were represented by others, and sometimes represented themselves, as 'naturalists', *phusikoi*, derived from *phusis*, nature (or alternatively as *phusiologoi*, those concerned with the account, *logos*, of *phusis*). Their writings were often labelled 'Concerning Nature', *peri phuseōs*, though in some cases that may not have been the original title the authors themselves gave them. In one case, that of Gorgias, his damning critique of the very possibility of any knowledge or communication about what is and indeed whether anything could be said to exist was nevertheless entitled 'On What Is Not or On Nature'.[1] His three-part thesis in this work was that nothing exists, but that if it exists, it is unknowable, and that if it exists and is knowable, it still cannot be indicated to others.

Ideas about what 'natural phenomena' comprised varied, as did opinions concerning how far they could indeed be explained and how to go about that. Heraclitus was already quoted as saying that 'nature loves to hide' (Fr. 123), a theme that Hadot (2006) made much of in his explorations of attitudes to the mysteries of nature in post-Aristotelian thought. But while different brands of scepticism were, as we shall see, articulated from time to time in the Graeco-Roman world, on the other side a more confident and positive view was commonly assumed and expressed. The naturalists

---

[1] An earlier Presocratic philosopher, a follower of the monist Parmenides, namely Melissus, is reported to have entitled his work 'On Nature or What Is'.

thought they could explain a vast array of phenomena, ranging from the movements of the heavenly bodies and meteorological phenomena such as lightning and thunder, earthquakes, winds and whirlwinds, through to animals, plants, minerals and stones. Ordinary folk might be baffled, even frightened, but they, the naturalists, could give regular explanations. The claim to be experts in the matter is obvious and what generated the introduction of the master concept 'nature' itself.

The explanation of the causes of diseases similarly exercised many of the fifth- and fourth-century BCE medical writers represented in the so-called Hippocratic Corpus, who insisted on the one hand that every disease had a natural cause, but also, on the other, that to be diseased was 'against nature', when the natural was equated with the healthy. What 'health' consisted in was construed differently by different thinkers (Lloyd 2003), but we can notice already a certain tension between a descriptive and an evaluative or normative use of 'nature'. Sometimes that term referred to what is the case, but on occasion it is used of an ideal, as often in what Aristotle claimed to be 'natural'. Thus Aristotle defined 'right' as the side from which movement begins and even put it that this is by nature most correctly exemplified in human beings, so that our 'right' is 'most right-sided' (*Progression of Animals* 706a19ff.). Analogously, 'up' is defined in relation to the place from which food is distributed and from which growth begins. So the 'upper' portion of plants will be where their roots are: accordingly plants are 'upside down' (e.g. *Parts of Animals* 686b31ff.). Meanwhile, one major group of topics debated across philosophy and medicine was what physical things in general were made of, their physical constitution; that is, the elements from which they came and the compounds those elements formed.

An alternative focus for the Greek philosophers' attention, ethics, figured less prominently at the beginning. Cicero's statement (*Tusculan Disputations* 5.4.10) that it was Socrates who 'brought philosophy down from the heavens' may be somewhat exaggerated but is generally accepted as very roughly correct. Certainly Plato represents him, in the *Phaedo* (96a ff.), as turning away from his earlier interest in natural phenomena to the study of intelligible objects, where of course he was especially concerned with virtue, a major preoccupation with Plato himself even though he also produced a detailed account of cosmology in his *Timaeus*.

Aristotle's extensive natural-philosophical works came equipped with their own methodology. He was careful to distinguish the methods proper for different inquiries, partly in terms of their subject matter, partly in that of the degree of exactness to be expected. While 'first philosophy' (metaphysics) deals with what is necessary, 'physics' – that is, the study of nature as he construed it – concerns what is true 'always or for the most part'. Again ethics cannot be expected to be as exact as mathematics. In the *Nicomachean Ethics* 1094b12 ff. he famously insists that

> the same degree of precision should not be demanded in all inquiries . . . Fine and just actions, which are the subject matter of politics, admit of plenty of differences and variations . . . It is as inappropriate to demand demonstration in ethics as it is to allow a mathematician to use merely probable arguments.

Yet there are overlaps, in Aristotle's account of intellectual disciplines, notably between 'physics' and ethics. We noted in chapter 2 one important example where the concept of 'nature' is in play in his ethical and political works, namely when he defines a human as 'by nature' a *politikon zōon*. Again, when Aristotle discusses modes of exchange he contrasts the 'natural' character of barter with other 'necessary' modes of exchange that depend on money (*Politics* 1257a33 ff.). Notoriously he maintains that the contrast between ruling and being ruled is natural and that some humans are natural slaves (while he recognises that some humans have been forced into slavery, *Politics* 1255a4 ff. Cf. Lloyd 1996b, ch. 9).

After Aristotle a conventional tripartite division of philosophy into logic, ethics and physics was generally adopted even by those who mounted sceptical arguments concerning the very possibility of giving causal explanations of hidden reality or obscure phenomena. Meanwhile the positive answers that were given about the constitution of things by Stoics, Epicureans and others differed widely. Continuum theorists who postulated that matter is infinitely divisible were locked in controversy with atomists in disputes that were never to be resolved and that were indeed to be exploited by those who claimed they never could be.

Now as I have argued on other occasions (Lloyd 1996a: 6–7), Chinese thinkers before the advent of Western influence had no exact equivalent to the Greek term *phusis* or our 'nature'. So the question of how they represented their work and what they thought it was possible and right to investigate is an important one where we must clearly not bring to bear in our answers our own conceptual assumptions, in many cases a legacy from those ancient Greeks. I shall take as my prime source the admittedly exceptional set of writings that goes by the name of the *Zhuangzi*. But before I embark on that, a word or two must be said on a quite promising area where some direct comparisons can be made between Greek and Chinese preoccupations. This is in the interest shown in the topic of the origins of things, in other words in what we call cosmogony.

Yet even here we have to be careful for we cannot assume that the 'cosmos' that is thus generated has the same general characteristics for the major Greek and Chinese thinkers who discussed how it came to be. In particular we can observe one important difference in the end result of the cosmogonical process in that the Greeks tended to think of the cosmos itself as a matter of a stable order between well-defined substances, while in ancient China the order is more generally one of interactive processes. It would clearly be foolish and indeed quite anachronistic to attempt an overall assessment of these two by trying to determine which compares more closely with modern thinking. Rather, the lesson we shall need to take away from our analysis is that alternative frameworks provide different possibilities for cosmological exploration.

Where, as just noted, the Greeks argued about the elements of things, the Chinese focused on the interactions of the five 'phases' (*wu xing*). This notion of five phase transformations probably originated in a theory of dynastic change (Sivin in Lloyd and Sivin 2002: 263–4). We find evidence of this in the text known as the *Lüshi chunqiu* put together around 215 BCE on the orders of Lü Buwei, who was prime minister to the man who was to become the First Emperor, Qin Shi Huang Di. At 13/2/1 the Yellow Emperor represents a series of dynastic changes as following the so-called mutual conquest order of the five phases, starting with earth (yellow), wood (green), metal (white), fire (red) and water (black), the last being associated with the rise of the state of Qin itself. Another later compilation, the *Huainanzi*, composed under the auspices of Liu An, the King of Huainan and uncle of the Han Emperor Wu Di, around 135 BCE, provides clear statements both of the mutual production order (water, wood, fire, earth, metal, *Huainanzi* ch. 3: 28b) and of the mutual conquest one (wood overcomes earth, which overcomes water, which overcomes fire, which overcomes metal which overcomes wood to restart the cycle; *Huainanzi* ch. 4: 11a). We can begin to make sense of this starting from some mundane examples. Water does indeed extinguish fire and fire melts metal. Again water helps to produce wood when trees grow, and fire, burned to ash, produces earth. But as we shall see, the phases are not the names of substances so much as of processes.

It so happens that three of these phases, translated 'water', 'fire' and 'earth', are the usual names for three of the Aristotelian simple bodies.[2] But this is quite deceptive, for what Chinese meant by 'water' (*shui*) is far

---

[2] A theory of four primary elements, that he called 'roots', occurs first in Empedocles and was taken over by many other Greeks, including in Plato's cosmology, although he gives them a geometrical interpretation, correlating them with four of the regular geometrical solids.

from identical to the Greeks' understanding of *hudōr*. The key point is well known. For Aristotle water, defined as cold and wet, is an irreducible element, or rather simple body. For Chinese cosmologists water is linked to fire and earth in a mutual conquest cycle, and to metal and wood in a cycle of mutual production. It is the name of the liquid we drink and that flows in rivers, but more properly it is conceived as a process.

Chinese texts make this perspective clear and enable us to see how different this is from Greek speculations. As the *Hong Fan* chapter in the *Shang Shu* (Book of Documents, Karlgren 1950: 28 and 30) puts it, 'Water means (*yue*) soaking downwards. Fire means flaming upwards. Wood means bending and straightening. Metal means conforming and changing. Earth means accepting seed and giving crops'. The focus here is clearly on processes and potential, not on elementary substances and their compounds.[3] At the same time the association of different things enables correlations and correspondences to be built up that serve as a framework for a general picture of the universe as a whole, not just physical objects but also the seasons, tastes, smells, colours, the emotions and social roles and institutions in a vast tableau of what has been dubbed 'correlative thinking'.[4] Yet it evidently did not require a focus on nature to appreciate the connectivity of things. Let us remember that while the Greeks were aware of the mutual attraction of magnetised iron, it was the Chinese who eventually discovered the directionality of the magnet.

Then another significant difference emerges from a further passage in the compilation I have already mentioned. When the *Lüshi chunqiu* (1/2/2) speaks of the character (*xing*) of 'water', it identifies this as 'purity', being 'clear' (*qing*). When the text continues by saying that the *xing* of humans (*ren*) is 'long life' (*shou*) it becomes apparent that this author is not trying to define the physical nature of water and humanity but rather setting out an ideal in each case, the character of the thing in question when it is at its best. Similarly the famous dispute between Xunzi and two of his predecessors, Mencius (Mengzi) and Gaozi, on whether humans are good, bad or indifferent, which is couched in terms of how to describe their *xing*, is not about their physical characteristics, but rather their moral ones.[5]

---

[3] This chapter has been dated to the third century BCE and is discussed by Graham (1989: 326), Nylan (2001: 239–41) and Lloyd and Sivin (2002: 259–60).

[4] See, for example, Needham 1956: 262 ff. and cf. Graham 1986 and 1989: 340 ff.; and Unschuld 1985: 65 ff. Although the focus on correlations is shared by many classical Chinese texts, the actual associations proposed vary considerably and exhibit some inconsistencies.

[5] See Mencius 6A/6 and *Xunzi* 23 (*xing e*); cf. Graham 1989: 117 ff., 244 ff.

One of the more comprehensive accounts of the origins of things comes from the other text I have already cited, namely the *Huainanzi*. Chapter 3 opens with:

> when heaven and earth were not yet formed, all was floating and flying, cavernous and unformed. Thus it was called the Great Beginning. The Dao proceeded to engender the vast emptinesses. The vast emptinesses engendered space/time. Space/time produced the primordial *qi*, and they [the *qi*] had edges and boundaries. That which was light and bright [*yang*] dissipated and dispersed to form heaven. That which was heavy and turbid congealed and coagulated to form earth. It was easy for the light and subtle to combine and concentrate, but difficult for the heavy and turbid to congeal and compact. Thus the heaven was completed first and the earth fixed afterwards. The united essences of heaven and earth constituted *yin* and *yang*. The combined essences of *yin* and *yang* constituted the four seasons. The scattered essences of the four seasons constituted the myriad things.[6]

The theme is one of an initial state of undifferentiation – just as it was in many Greek accounts, such as that attributed to Anaximander, who similarly engaged in some heady speculations about how the cosmogonic process works. Here in the *Huainanzi* heaven and earth[7] are what is first differentiated, the latter associated with *yin* and the former with *yang*, and there are many other texts that focus on the primordial separation of *yin* and *yang*. Thus when the *Lüshi chunqiu* discusses the 'Great Music', it says that the Great One brings forth the Dyadic Couple, which in turn bring forth *yin* and *yang*, which metamorphose and transform, rising and falling, eventually producing the 'myriad things', *wanwu*.[8] Usually no external agency is described at work:[9] the processes are spontaneous, for which the ordinary Chinese term is *ziran*, literally 'self-so'. That is, they are 'natural' in the sense that there was no external intervention, though in the account of the end product, the emphasis is on its variety, not on any unifying character it or they may display.

The *Zhuangzi* presents a very different picture and indeed poses formidable problems of interpretation. The text that has come down to us is an amalgam of writings from different periods from the fourth to

---

[6] *Huainanzi* ch. 3: 1a. There are several obscurities in the detail of this text, although the main thrust of the argument is clear. Compare the translations in Major 1993: 62, somewhat modified in Major et al. 2010: 114–15, and that in Le Blanc and Matthieu 2003: 101–2.

[7] That is, the mass of earth, *di*, that is formed under the heavens, rather than the process or phase that we translate as 'earth', i.e. soil, in the conception of the cyclical transformations of the five phases, where the graph is different, namely *tu*.

[8] *Lüshi chunqiu* 5/2/1; Knoblock and Riegel 2000: 136.

[9] Cf. Goldin 2008, who surveys the evidence for cosmogonic myths in ancient China.

the second centuries BCE. The purported author, Zhuang Zhou himself, appears as a figure in the account of different ideas about the Dao that is given in the final chapter (*tian xia*, ch. 33) of the compilation, where indeed his ideas are criticised as extravagant and abstruse, even though (like the other thinkers discussed) he 'got wind of' part of the 'ancient tradition of the Way and delighted in it' (33: 63–9). Evidently those criticisms come from a particular layer in the tradition of the transmission of these texts. Given that one of the recurrent themes throughout the work is the problem of inexpressibility, or at least the acute difficulties of communication, and another the inadequacies or shortcomings of language in conveying meaning (a topic to which I shall return in chapter 5), we must recognise that our own understanding of what this text has to offer us is bound to be both limited and precarious.[10]

We may nevertheless pick up certain salient and recurrent themes that give us some indication of how these writings represent what it is that they are dealing with. A passage in the *qiwulun* chapter (2) gives us a starting point. A contrast is drawn (2: 3–8) between hearing 'the pipes of man (humans)', hearing the 'pipes of earth' and hearing the 'pipes of heaven', where the three modes of listening are graded in difficulty and importance. We are encouraged to believe that enlightenment can be achieved, though it is certainly no straightforward matter. Here and often elsewhere, heaven, *tian*, is evidently the prime target. As such it has often been glossed as corresponding to some concept of 'nature'. But any such identification soon runs into difficulties. The first is that heaven is often (as here) contrasted with earth, where heaven is thought of as superior to earth. So some interpreters retreat from a simple identification of heaven with nature and instead identify the pair heaven and earth (*tiandi*) as such. But while the Greeks generally also assumed the superiority, even the divinity, of the heavens, they entertained a notion of an inquiry into *phusis* that covered everything that is or can be in motion.[11]

When heaven is said to be circular, and earth square, we can certainly call this cosmography. The latter idea corresponds to the common ancient Chinese assumption of a flat earth with the Middle Kingdom in the centre surrounded by the four seas. Quite how the heavens were to be represented

[10] Li 2015 undertakes a careful recent analysis both of the difficulties of interpreting the *Zhuangzi* texts and of the positive messages they convey on both cosmological and ethical questions.

[11] Of course, as I shall be discussing in chapter 4, Aristotle maintained that the heavens were ontologically distinct, made of a different stuff, *aithēr*, a fifth element quite unlike the four sublunary ones, and he certainly associated the heavens with what is divine. Yet as the inquiry that deals with everything in motion, the heavens included, 'physics' is a single unified subject.

was the subject of some dispute, for the notion of a 'canopy heaven' (*gai tian*) was opposed to one of an 'enveloping heaven' (*hun tian*).[12] Adopting the former model, the *Zhoubi suanjing*, composed around the turn of the millennium, engaged in some detailed investigations attempting quantitative results for the dimensions of the earth and the height of the sun.[13] There are no such inquiries in the *Zhuangzi*, which, like many other texts, simply contents itself by saying that the heaven circles and covers everything, while the earth is firm and supports things.

Yet in *Zhuangzi*, as in other texts, there is far more to the use of *tian* than just as a term for what we see above our heads, the sky. The concept is also used in relation to destiny, of man's destiny in general and that of individual men or other creatures in particular.[14] Speaking of an exceptional person, ch. 3 (Graham 1981: 64) puts it, 'When heaven engenders something it causes it to be unique.' It is not that everyone necessarily fulfils their destiny (as it would, if their whole life was predetermined). You may or may not live out your quota of years. Many texts focus on what you have to do, or how you have to behave, for that to happen.[15] And similarly animals and plants may or may not get to live their full complement of years. Every creature should strive to do 'the work of heaven', but it is in no way guaranteed that they will succeed.

There is a tension indeed between 'the work of heaven' and 'the work of man'. To grasp the distinction is said to be key to complete knowledge (ch. 6, Graham 1981: 84), but its difficulty is underlined. At first sight it might be tempting to equate the work of heaven with physics and that of man with ethics. But the text goes on to problematise these knowings and indeed the distinction between them. It is very easy to confuse heaven's doing with man's. Besides, heaven's point of view is radically different from that of man, even though it is emphasised how difficult the former is to attain. Still we are warned (ch. 6, Graham 1981: 90) that 'extraordinary men are extraordinary in the eyes of men but ordinary in the eyes of Heaven. As

---

[12] In the *gai tian* view the heaven is a circular canopy set over a central square earth. In the *hun tian* model the heavens are spherical, with half of the sphere invisible below the earth at any given time. Each view was associated with particular observational techniques and instruments, the gnomon and the armillary sphere respectively. See Cullen 1996: 35–66.

[13] On the basis of the assumption of a flat central earth this treatise uses gnomon shadow differences to come up with concrete answers to such questions as the height and distance of the sun (23.4 ff.: see Cullen 1996: 176 ff.). A similar technique is used in *Huainanzi* 3: see Cullen 1993 and Volkov 1996–7: 145–58.

[14] In *Huainanzi* 1: 12a we read, 'that an ox has cloven hooves and grows horns, and that a horse has a mane and square hooves, is heaven. But to put a bit in the horse's mouth and a ring in the ox's nose is human.'

[15] This is a theme in *Zhuangzi* ch. 4 (Graham 1981: 74), ch. 6 (Graham 1981: 84) and ch. 27, which I shall be considering in some detail in a moment.

the saying goes: "Heaven's knave is man's gentleman, man's gentleman is heaven's knave"'.

Where the Greek cosmologists generally assumed that nature, reality, the cosmos, existed independently of the observer and were a proper subject of investigation, the *Zhuangzi* texts look out on a world that challenges, even at points defeats, understanding. We try to make definite statements, announcing that 'that's it' or 'that is not' as the case may be.[16] But any such statements are destabilised. *Zhuangzi* ch. 2, 27–30, puts it, 'No thing is not "other": no thing is not "it"'. 'What is "it" is also "other", what is "other" is also "it". There they say "that's it, that's not" from one point of view. Here we say "that's it, that is not" from another point of view'. All that we are entitled to is remarks that rely on and acknowledge the perspective from which they are made.

A remarkable chapter (*yu yan*, 'lodge sayings', ch. 27) makes some telling points about different types of discourse that have wide-ranging implications for persuasion and inter-personal communication in general. It offers a three-part classification of ways of saying, namely 'lodge-sayings', 'weighty sayings' and 'spill-over sayings' (27: 1–5). There is much that is obscure, and points to which I can do less than justice here. Thus the commentators take 'spill-over sayings' to derive their name from a kind of vessel that is designed to tip and right itself when it is filled too near the brim. 'Use it to go by', the text says, 'and let the stream find its own channels: this is the way to last out your years', which Graham (1989: 201) rather optimistically glosses as 'the speech proper to the intelligent spontaneity of Taoist [that is, Daoist] behaviour in general, a fluid language which keeps its equilibrium through changing meanings and viewpoints'.

However, as regards the other two types of discourse, 'weighty sayings', which are what you say on your own authority, are less effective in persuasion than 'lodge sayings'. The former work seven times out of ten, while the latter do so nine times out of ten. The crucial point is that these are sayings where you 'borrow a standpoint outside to sort the matter out'. The 'lodging-place' is the position of the other party in the debate, and the point is that you temporarily adopt that in order to win him over. As in ch. 2, so here in ch. 27, statements should not be judged independently of the perspective from which they are made.[17]

---

[16] This is expressed by way of the contrast between *shi* and *fei*. But those two terms are used not only for assertions ('it is') and denials ('it is not'), but also for right and wrong. So difficulties concerning definite affirmations spill over into those about values in particular.

[17] The account of 'lodge sayings' has sometimes been invoked in attempts to identify an indigenous Chinese linguistic category that corresponds to 'metaphor'. But the flaws in such an interpretation are not just a matter of what we are told about that discourse, but also of how it relates to the other

Does the overriding message of these various discussions in *Zhuangzi* amount to a radical undermining of all communication and to a consummate scepticism? The emphasis on the difficulties of knowing and of drawing categorical distinctions between things is certainly strong. Thus *Zhuangzi* ch. 2, 64–70, contains a dialogue between Nie Que ('Gaptooth') and Wang Ni. 'Gaptooth' asks him, 'would you know something where all are agreed?' To which Wang Ni replies, 'how would I know that?' The next question is, 'would you know that you did not know?' to which the answer is again, 'how would I know that?' 'Then does no thing know anything?' Yet again Wang Ni replies, 'how would I know that?' but he has a shot, nevertheless, at explaining that for different creatures what causes pain, what is edible and what is beautiful differs. So 'the paths of "that's it" and "that's not" are inextricably confused.'

Nevertheless the texts have much to say on how one should behave, not being taken in by what is customarily valued nor by what is customarily feared (death in particular). And if definite assertions about how things are should be avoided, much is said about the possibility of knowing through practising. Cooks, carpenters, engravers, archers are frequently invoked for their genuine skills in doing what they are good at, where the tacit point is sometimes that this is not knowledge that can be put into words.[18] Knowing <u>how</u>, we might say, is not subject to the damning critique that knowing <u>that</u> is subjected to. Saying, we are told, positively, is not just 'blowing breath' (*Zhuangzi* ch. 2: 23): communication is taking place, however difficult it is to interpret what is communicated. Clearly, following the lead of these texts, we have to be extremely cautious of the claims that we make. We may be able to hear 'the pipes of man', but there are the pipes of earth and then those of heaven that may well be beyond the reach of anyone who has not yet achieved sagehood (and that means all of us).

The *Zhuangzi* texts delight in the elusive, the anecdotal, the paradoxical, the apparently flatly self-contradictory, and we are repeatedly faced with

two modes of saying, neither of which singly, nor the two in combination, can be said to come close to giving us a category that corresponds to the usual antonym of 'metaphor', namely the literal. We have here a classic example of the mistakes that arise from the imposition of Western categories on Chinese materials.

[18] See, for example, the discussion of the great skill of Cook Ding in *Zhuangzi* ch. 3, that of the wheelwright Bian in ch. 13, and that of the engraver Qing in ch. 19. In the last case, when Qing is asked by the Marquis of Lu what his secret is, he replies, 'Your servant is just an artisan, what secret could he have?' However, he explains that before making a bell-stand he first fasts: outside distractions fade away and only then does he go into the forests to see how heaven makes the wood grow. 'The aptitude of the body attains its peak . . . only then do I put my hand to it . . . So I join what is heaven's to what is heaven's. Would this be the reason why the instrument seems daemonic [i.e. possessed of extraordinary spiritual power]?' (Graham 1981: 135).

the problem of discerning what, if anything indeed, the author or authors themselves might be committed to, bearing in mind that that commitment is no more than a 'relying on from a certain perspective'. Obviously there is no encouragement here to undertake what we may call empirical research into natural phenomena. The contrast with Aristotle when he composed his passionate protreptic to the detailed study of animals in *On the Parts of Animals* I chs. 1 and 5, is stark.[19] Yet the *Zhuangzi* texts do not just relapse into quietism or limit themselves to some council of despair. Rather, they set as an aim listening to those pipes, of humans, of the earth and especially of heaven. In other words, they encourage deep reflection on how things are in order to achieve some understanding that will enable us to be in tune with the universe.

Two further anecdotes, both involving interactions between Zhuang Zhou and his friend and sparring partner Hui Shi,[20] will illustrate the two essential points, the negative one of the futility of a certain kind of inquisitiveness and the positive one of the importance of being in harmony with the world. In the final chapter (33: 69), Hui Shi is said to have 'many formulae: his writings filled five carts, but his Way was eccentric', full of notorious paradoxes indeed, such as 'the dimensionless cannot be accumulated, yet its girth is 1,000 leagues'.

> Hui Shi's chatter seemed to him supremely clever . . . There was a strange man of the South called Huang Lao, who asked why heaven does not collapse or earth subside, and the causes of wind, rain and thunder. Hui Shi answered without hesitation, replied without thinking, had explanations for all the myriad things, never stopped explaining, said more and more, and still thought he had not said enough, had some marvel to add . . . What a pity that Hui Shi's talents were wasted, and never came to anything, that he would not turn back from chasing the myriad things! He had as much

[19] Aristotle there contrasts the study of the heavenly bodies with that of things on earth. The former is more precious, since they are divine, but the latter, the study of plants and animals, has the advantage in that we have access to greater information about them. 'For anyone who is willing to take sufficient trouble can learn a great deal concerning each one of their kinds.' We should, then, investigate every kind of animal, 'without, as far as possible, omitting any one of them, but dealing with noble and ignoble alike. For even in those that are not attractive to the senses, yet to the intellect the craftsmanship of nature provides extraordinary pleasures for those who can recognise the causes in things and who are naturally inclined to philosophy . . . So we must not feel a childish disgust at the investigation of the meaner animals. For there is something of the marvellous in all natural things . . . In each one of them there is something natural and something beautiful.' *On the Parts of Animals* I ch. 5, 644b22–645a23.

[20] *Zhuangzi* ch. 33 is our main source for a series of paradoxes proposed by Hui Shi, whose own writings are not extant. He is regularly pigeonholed as a leader of the so-called School of Names (*Ming Jia*). But for all his interests in logical conundrums, Hui Shi was, like most other ancient Chinese philosophers, also involved in advising rulers and is even reported to have drawn up a code of laws for the state of Wei (*Lüshi chunqiu* 18/5/8).

chance of making his voice outlast its echo, his body outrun its shadow. Sad, wasn't it? (*Zhuangzi* ch. 33: 80–7, Graham 1981: 284–5)

Of course this passage can be taken as evidence that, exceptionally, some Chinese thinkers were interested in giving causal explanations of the phenomena in much the same way as the Presocratics and many later Greek thinkers were. At the same time it shows that such investigations cut no ice where the *Zhuangzi* authors are concerned. Yet my second anecdote illustrates where those authors nevertheless convey a positive message which does value reflection on how things are, understanding and being in tune (as I put it) with the universe.

Zhuangzi ch. 18 speaks of what happened when Zhuang Zhou's wife died. Hui Shi arrives on a visit of condolence, only to find Zhuang Zhou squatting, drumming on a pot and singing. At which Hui Shi says it would be bad enough, having lived with someone and grown old together, to refuse to mourn her death, 'but to drum on a pot and sing, could there be anything more shameful?' 'Not so', Zhuang Zhou replies.

> When she first died, do you suppose I was able not to feel the loss? I peered back into her beginnings; there was a time before there was a life. Not only was there no life, there was a time before there was a shape. Not only was there no shape, there was a time before there was energy (*qi*). Mingled together in the amorphous, something altered, and there was the energy; by alteration in the energy there was the shape, by alteration in the shape there was the life. Now once more altered she has gone over to death. That is to be companion with spring and autumn, summer and winter, in the procession of the four seasons. When someone was about to lie down in the greatest of mansions, I with my sobbing knew no better than to bewail her. The thought came to me that I was being uncomprehending towards destiny, so I stopped. (*Zhuangzi* ch. 18: 15–19, trans. Graham 1989: 175–6 modified)

Let me now draw the threads of my discussion in this chapter together and recapitulate its main findings, where I must start by reiterating my customary caveat about the difficulty of generalising about all or even most Greek or Chinese thinkers as a whole. In both ancient societies many different points of view were expressed on the world around us and humans' place in it, on what is worthwhile investigating and on values more generally. Each society produced on the one hand sceptics and critics of different shades, as well as, on the other, those who offered more positive answers to the questions they considered important.[21]

---

[21] Lloyd and Sivin 2002 discuss what it was for individual thinkers to belong to sects or schools in either ancient society. Some, though not all, Chinese *jia* (lineages, literally 'families') had an official

The first and fundamental point I have insisted on is that while the Greeks adopted the wide-ranging, ambivalent and at points ambiguous concept of nature as the principal focus of their cosmological and physical investigations, there is no exact equivalent to that in ancient China. Yet we find there too a good deal of interest first in the origins of things – cosmogony, in other words – second in the relations between heaven and earth – cosmography – and third in the cycles of the changes and transformations of things and in the correspondences and associations that link everything in the universe together. In all three contexts Chinese writers accumulated a good deal of robust knowledge concerning particular phenomena and processes, though they did not do so in the name of the inquiry into nature nor in a bid to show that they had special expertise in any such domain.

Then a fourth topic of major Chinese concern is the relations between heaven, earth and man. We tend to call their ideas on such links macrocosm–microcosm 'analogies' (which is what they are in ancient Greece, when the human body is construed as like the cosmos).[22] But in China they are in fact more than just parallelisms, in the respect that heaven, earth and man (both the human body and the political state) form a seamless whole. Sivin showed in detail (Lloyd and Sivin 2002: 214 ff.)[23] how the political state is understood as a cosmos, and so too the living body. Body, state, earth, heaven, form a seamless whole. All exhibit the same basic structure – all manifest the interactions of *yin* and *yang*.

If these Chinese cosmological ideas incorporate important value judgements and lessons for morality, we should recall that in Greece too *phusis* plays a role not just in the subject called 'the inquiry into nature' but also in ethics and politics. Given the interests of Chinese 'wandering persuaders',[24] there is nothing surprising in the fact that sooner or later we generally

role in the education of the ruling elite. Most Greek *haireseis* were private organisations. What they all had in common, in both China and the Graeco-Roman world, was *some* degree of allegiance to handing on some teaching associated either with an individual or with a text or texts.

[22] The fifth-century BCE atomist Democritus is reported as having first represented the human being as a *mikros kosmos* (Frr. 4, 5, 34). Some of the most elaborate examples of such speculations come in the Hippocratic writers, most notably *On Regimen* and *On Sevens* (the latter of very uncertain date) (Lloyd 1966: 252–3). However, the most influential statement of the thesis that the cosmos itself is a living creature was in Plato's *Timaeus*, though a similar view was to be taken up and made much of by the Stoics.

[23] The key texts that Sivin passes under review come from the *Lüshi chunqiu* (3/5/1–2 and 20/5/1) and the medical classic *Huangdi neijing* (*ling shu* 1/6/265, *tai su* 3/31/3 and 19/21/3 and *su wen* 8/1–2/28). There are three main recensions of this work for which we depend on eighth-century CE editions. But much of the contents of the *ling shu* and *su wen* at least can be dated to the first century BCE.

[24] Many of those whom we customarily think of as Chinese 'philosophers' were such 'wandering persuaders', for which the usual Chinese term is *you shui*.

encounter a focus on the overriding importance of order and good government, on the proper relations among humans, between kings and ministers, parents and children, males and females. To know how to behave properly – even for the iconoclastic *Zhuangzi* – means understanding the universe – cosmology in that sense – even while that understanding includes recognising the limits of what can be understood.

In both ancient societies the ultimate importance of understanding the cosmos lies in that it enables you to live a life in tune with it, a matter, therefore, of no mere intellectual comprehension. True, some Greeks, notably Aristotle, claimed that theoretical knowledge was valuable for its own sake. Yet he certainly represented the pay-off in terms of our happiness, while his Hellenistic successors saw the reward as freedom from anxiety, *ataraxia*. For those later Greeks the ethical goal depended up to a point on physics – for if you did not understand natural phenomena you were likely to be afraid of them and that would destroy your peace of mind. But without a programme of 'physics' as such, we see that a sense of awareness of where things originate and the forces they respond to is an essential component of the vision that many Chinese had of the Dao.

My thesis has been that the Chinese texts we have discussed show how it is possible to do cosmology without a concept of nature, and what kind of cosmology results. But two possible objections to my line of argument must be considered in conclusion. The first is that, even if there is no single explicit equivalent to 'nature' or *phusis* in classical Chinese texts, those texts manifest at least a clear implicit grasp of such a concept, so that I have exaggerated the difference between the two programmes. The second is that my discussion of Greek *phusis* itself underestimates its ambivalence.

As regards the first point, I would of course concede that the Chinese – like everyone else – appreciated many of the regularities in what we – and the ancient Greeks – call 'natural' phenomena, the changes in the seasons, the way plants grow and animals reproduce and much else besides. But it is important nevertheless to emphasise first that while 'regularity' may be a necessary condition for what is considered 'natural', it is certainly not a sufficient one, for plenty of regularities do not belong to 'nature' at all, but to custom or convention: religious festivals and socially sanctioned modes of behaviour would be two examples. Second, we must bear in mind that while the Chinese had available different concepts that do well enough to capture aspects of what we consider to be 'natural', the fact that the concepts differ, and that so too do the contexts in which they appear, is important. We have seen how *tian*, heaven, is used in one context, the spontaneous (*ziran*) in another, and character (*xing*) in a third, and to those one could add *wanwu* (the myriad things), *li* (the patterns of things) and even the Dao itself. But these are not mere variations on a single theme, for the differences between these concepts and the issues they address are significant. The Chinese were not tempted to run them all together, to support some idea that they all relate to one and the same problematic, namely 'nature'. Whether the Greeks were wise to tend to do just that is very much open to debate. The Chinese experience should serve, indeed, to cast doubt on that, for it illustrates the possibility of an alternative understanding of the explananda and of the proper modes of explanation.

That takes me then to the second objection, which was that the Greek concept itself is even more polyvalent than I allowed. Again I would concede and actually insist first that *phusis* manifests exceptional semantic stretch, and second that the ancient Greeks themselves were locked in dispute about the nature of 'nature'. So far from homogenising their views on the subject, I have endeavoured to show how their disagreements provide us with an important clue as to the way their speculations developed. It was in their contests for prestige that the importance of a concept of nature as such came to be worked out. The aim of those involved was to impose a conception, their own conception, of what the domain of 'physics' comprised, thereby bolstering their particular claims to be considered the acknowledged experts in the domain.

If both these objections can be met and answered, the upshot of our examination of ancient speculations in this chapter still stands. Negatively we should not assume (if we ever did) that, starting with the Greeks, the West has some monopoly in the matter of the correct ideas on what there is to investigate and on how to carry out that inquiry. If the Chinese can be said to do cosmology without nature, by parity of reasoning we could say that the ancient Greeks do so without the concept of *yin* and *yang*. We should not, in other words, suppose that beyond a certain point a cosmological investigation necessarily has to follow a single pattern or define its proper subject matter in a particular way.

More positively we can make the most of the pluralism and heterogeneity of the views and aspirations for which our ancient records provide evidence. In some respects this mirrors the findings of the anthropologists we discussed in chapter 2, even while we should also note certain divergences. We have brought to light some remarkable contrasts within and between two societies that Descola both considered examples of analogism, on the basis of the assumptions of physicality and interiority that underpin their ontological regimes. The ancient Greek philosophers we have analysed shared with modern 'naturalists' an assumption that there is a single determinate and determinable reality ('nature') that should be the unique target of inquiry. Some Chinese ones more readily accepted that different views reflected different perspectives, and Zhuangzi certainly held that all depend on *some* perspective.

That in turn is reminiscent of the perspectivism discussed by Viveiros de Castro, though that extends more radically beyond humans to include the perspectives also of non-human beings. Yet the point that marks out both Chinese and Greek wrestling with the problems is the degree of articulateness of the positions they advocated in explicit dialogue with contemporaries and predecessors. I shall be returning to the relevance and impact of literacy in chapter 5, but for now should underline that Zhuangzi's perspectivism reflects a distinct view of the nature of language and of the status of any assertion and denial.

Meanwhile, the main lesson we take away from our forays into ancient history relates to the pluralism I have mentioned. The thinkers in both ancient societies I have concentrated on were deeply concerned with giving some account of the world around them, of the place of humans in it, of the limits of possible human understanding and of how best we should live. Yet their ideas both of the nature of the questions and of how to answer them exhibit considerable diversity. That should give us pause if, in the wake of the Greeks, we may still be beguiled into assuming there is a single reality that poses a well-defined problem capable of definitive solution. This is a theme I shall pursue further in my next chapter, where I shall take as my particular focus the fortunes of the dichotomy between Being and mere Seeming to be.

CHAPTER 4

Seeming and Being

Binary oppositions, often originating in Greek antiquity, have attracted a good deal of critical attention in the last few decades, most notably from Derrida (e.g. 1982), but the character of the binaries under attack and the relations between the opposed terms vary considerably. We cannot afford to ignore both the logical and the substantial differences between the following highly contested oppositions: nature versus nurture or culture or the artificial, demonstration versus persuasion, reason versus perception, mind as opposed to body, the analytic versus the synthetic, the a priori versus the a posteriori, the literal versus the metaphorical, the contrast between convergers and divergers (Hudson 1966), between the masculine mind and the feminine (Baron-Cohen 2003), or even masculinity and femininity themselves, between causal accounts and correlative ones, competition and co-operation, realism and relativism, Being and Seeming.

In every case understandings both of the character of each disjunct and of the relationship between them have been challenged, modified, even debunked, and in several instances I have elaborated some of the necessary revisions in this set of studies here. It turns out, over and over again, that what were sometimes construed as mutually exclusive and in many cases exhaustive alternatives are nothing of the kind. When that is so, to insist on a choice between the two alternatives is to force some issue, to leave out of account the complexity of the concepts in question, the possibility, sometimes, of combining them, or of finding options that the original binary masks or ignores. It also turns out, again and again, that those who introduced the contrast used it in polemic, in two ways especially, first to downgrade one half of the binary in favour of the other, and second and more especially to claim special expertise in the matter of the understanding of the binary itself. We have seen examples of this in the last chapter in relation to nature and to what I dub the master binary that we are concerned with, namely rationality and the irrational, and the present study will enable us to throw further light on the issues.

Picking up the theme of reality from the last chapter, I shall take as my chief topic here Seeming and Being themselves, aiming to explore some of the different ways in which that pair has been invoked, the limitations of its usefulness and the dangers of certain common assumptions about its applicability. The pair formed, of course, the main articulating framework in Plato's metaphysics, but it antedates him in Greek thought, having a variety of roles in Presocratic philosophy and indeed going back to our earliest Greek pre-philosophical texts, which is where we must begin. In Homer already a god or a goddess may take the form of some other creature, a human or a bird, for example. Some passages merely compare the gods with birds (for instance) (*Iliad* 5 778, 13 62, 15 237; *Odyssey* 5 51 f.) but in others the gods appear in the guise of birds (e.g. *Odyssey* 3 372; cf. 22 239 ff.). Again, gods can appear as humans and they can disguise humans to look more decrepit, or alternatively more beautiful and even godlike, than normal. So you can never be too sure. Appearances in these and other contexts can evidently be deceptive.

How the divine reveals itself is evidently problematic and uncertain. Is the bird a manifestation of the god or what conceals the godhead? There is even a difference, in Greek, in the constructions used with the verb *phainesthai* (to appear) that mirrors this ambiguity. When the verb is followed by a participle, we normally understand that the appearance tells us what something is, but when it governs a verb in the infinitive we read it as 'appears but is not really so'. Yet as the grammarians remind us, that general rule is far from always strictly adhered to, so there is always an element of doubt.

Hesiod, in turn, lays claim to much abstruse and esoteric knowledge in both the *Theogony* and the *Works and Days*, and he gives a story to justify this. His authority is the Muses, although he says that they know how to tell not just the truth but also many lies that are like the truth (*Theogony* 27–8). Hesiod assures his audience that he can tell the differences between auspicious and inauspicious days in the month for a whole range of human activities, but he remarks that there are few people who have knowledge of this (*Works* 822–5). Sometimes a day is a stepmother, sometimes a mother, as he puts it (825). The problem, by implication, is to distinguish between them in time and not mistake the one for the other. Initial appearances evidently may be deceptive.

From the start of their speculative inquiries the Presocratic philosophers devoted much of their energy, as we said, to attempting explanations of a wide variety of natural phenomena, especially, though not exclusively, those that were particularly striking or frightening – where they had generally been considered by their fellow Greeks to be signs of the work of the gods, of Zeus with his thunderbolt, for instance, or of Poseidon the earthshaker. For Anaximander, lightning and thunder were explained as due to wind, which, when enclosed in cloud, may burst out violently: then the tearing makes the sound and the rift brings about the lightning flash.[1] In a more elaborate example he proposed a theory of the heavenly bodies that explained their circular movement and occasional eclipses. He imagined the heavenly bodies as wheels of fire, enclosed in mist, which have vents through which the sun, moon or stars are visible. Eclipses occur when the vents temporarily become blocked.[2] A little later Xenophanes is quoted as saying (Fr. 32) that 'what people call Iris [the usual Greek name for the rainbow, though Iris was also imagined as the messenger of the gods], that too is a cloud, purple and scarlet and yellow to behold'. By treating it as a cloud, he naturalises it: we have no need to think of the rainbow as a portent, though that was not to say he persuaded all his fellow Greeks not to do so. At the same time he stays with the appearances: the rainbow with its special bright colours is different from other clouds. Those colours were not what we call optical illusions, as Aristotle seems to suppose with respect to some of the appearances of the rainbow.[3]

But of course many Presocratic explanations go far beyond the appearances. For Heraclitus, for whom, as we have seen, 'nature loves to hide' (Fr 123), the cosmos (world order) as a whole is an 'ever-living fire' (Fr. 30), not something we can be said to 'see'. True, he is also quoted as saying that 'those things of which there is sight, hearing, learning, they are what I privilege' (Fr. 55), but the addition of 'learning' (*mathēsis*) there shows that not all his evidence is perceptual, as indeed is also clear from his insistence that we should follow the *logos*, which is not a matter of what he says, but of the ratio or rule according to which everything comes to be.[4]

---

[1] This view is reported in the late source Aetius 3 3 1, though we should note that when Aristotle comes to review earlier theories of lightning and thunder in his *Meteorologica* book 2 ch. 9, he does not mention Anaximander.

[2] Again we rely on late sources, Hippolytus, *Refutation* 1 6 4, and Aetius 2 13 7, 2 20 1, 2 25 1. Anaximander is further reported as holding that the sun, moon and stars (in that order) are at regular distances, measured in earth-diameters, from the earth, with the stars being closest, the sun furthest away. Such a theory owes more to a desire for symmetry than to any empirical observation.

[3] In his *Meteorology* 371b33–372a10, Aristotle identifies three colours in the rainbow, roughly 'red' 'green' and 'blue', but he adds that there is often an appearance of 'yellow' between the 'red' and the 'green'. I use the conventional translations of Greek colour terms, although in many, indeed most, other contexts these refer not to hues but to luminosity (see Lloyd 2007a: ch. 1).

[4] What Heraclitus means by the *logos* is the key issue in the controversies that continue over the interpretation of his philosophy. In Fr. 50 he tells us to listen not to him, but to the *logos*. Fr. 2 describes it as common, although most people live as if they possessed their own wisdom. Fr. 1 from the start

By the middle of the fifth century BCE several Greek medical writers, responsible for some of the treatises in the Hippocratic Corpus, were also attempting theories and explanations, of diseases, of the structure and functioning of the human body and even, in some cases, of the constitution of physical objects as a whole. In the last example some based their accounts on elementary opposites such as hot, cold, wet and dry. On the one hand these qualities were in principle observable. On the other, that feature is subject to two major reservations. What might appear to be 'hot' may or may not be truly so. The true quality of an object was to be judged by its effects rather than by how we perceive it. Thus a cool alcoholic drink could be categorised as warming: a poisonous drug that was neither hot nor cold to the touch was nevertheless essentially 'cold'. So even those who, like Aristotle and much later Galen, stayed with a qualitative account of material objects (as opposed to the quantitative theories of the atomists) were faced with the basic difficulty of deciding what counts as 'hot' or 'cold' or 'wet' or 'dry'. Galen even introduced the idea of different grades of these qualities, corresponding, in the first case, not, of course, to degrees Celsius, but rather to the severity of their effects. Meanwhile for the atomists those qualities were to be accounted for by the properties of geometrical shapes taken singly or in combination, though Aristotle for one objected that to explain qualities in quantitative terms was a simple category mistake.

Then more generally the writer of the treatise *On Ancient Medicine* explicitly recognised that when some of his opponents invoked, as the causes of diseases, such primary qualities (hot, cold, wet, dry) as the constituents of the body, these were <u>theoretical</u> entities, 'postulates' or 'hypotheses', as he calls them, that were beyond verification. This writer says that medicine has no need of such 'hypotheses' and is in that respect unlike 'obscure and problematic subjects',

> concerning which anyone who attempts to hold forth at all is forced to use a hypothesis, as for example about things in the heaven or things under the earth: for if anyone were to speak and declare the nature of these things, it would not be clear either to the speaker himself or to his audience whether what was said was true or not, since there is no criterion to which one should refer to obtain clear knowledge.[5]

of his book claims that the *logos* is that according to which everything comes to be, while other fragments speak of the *logos* of the soul (Frr. 45, 115). At one end of the spectrum it covers words or speech, but at the other it is the objective rule or proportion governing physical changes (as in Fr. 31).

[5] *On Ancient Medicine* ch. 1, *CMG* I,1 36 15 ff.

Yet of course he himself goes beyond what can straightforwardly be observed when he tackles such problems as the effects of combinations of 'powers' in the body or those of the different structures of different parts in it. In the latter context he remarks that there are important differences between those structures. Some are 'hollow and tapering', some 'spread out', some 'hard and round', some 'dense', some 'loose and swollen', some 'spongy and porous', for instance. He poses the question for himself which type of structure is best suited to draw fluid to itself and answers the 'hollow and tapering' ones. 'One should learn these things outside the body from objects that are plain to see' (ch. 22, 53.12 f.).

This is one of several clear references to a methodological principle that probably goes back to Anaxagoras, according to which 'the phenomena [appearances] are the vision of what is obscure'.[6] Insofar as the 'vision' or understanding that is arrived at is a matter of the underlying nature or causes of the obscure objects or processes, the principle justifies a theoretical – that is, speculative – move. But insofar as the theory in question is based on the appearances, it appeals to some empirical support, not necessarily direct observable evidence, but at least some analogue to the explanandum, leaving, of course, the major problem of whether the positive analogies in question outweigh the differences between the explanandum and the model on which the explanation is constructed.[7]

Across the board, from philosophy to medicine, Greek writers already before Plato were trying out a variety of methodological justifications for their speculations, in most of which the appearances figure either as the objects to be explained or as the basis for some explanation. But at the opposite extreme, there is Parmenides' position radically undermining the appearances, in a move that goes far beyond raising a doubt or two about this or that phenomenon. He presents us with the contrast between the Way of Truth and a Way of Seeming or Opinion, Doxa.[8] The way of truth starts from the statement (Fr. 2) that 'it is and cannot not be' and proceeds to deduce a set of characteristics of what is. It is ungenerated and indestructible, not subject to any alteration or movement or change, for

---

[6] The dictum in this form is attributed by Sextus (*Against the Mathematicians* [*M*] 7 140) to Anaxagoras, and Sextus also says it was approved by Democritus. We find echoes of the dictum (with different nuances in its application) in the medical writers and even in Herodotus. The extensive secondary literature on the principle starts with Regenbogen 1930–1 and Diller 1932. Cf. Lloyd 1966: 338 ff.

[7] Cf. most recently Lloyd 2015, especially ch. 4.

[8] The Greek term *doxa* has a particularly wide semantic range. It may refer to seeming or opinion or judgement. The decisions taken in Greek assemblies were referred to as what was agreed by them, the verb being *dokei*, what seems good, but elsewhere where the contrast is with what is, what seems carries negative undertones. In another context, however, *doxa* may have a strong positive valence, as when it is used for 'fame' or 'reputation'.

to attribute any of those characteristics to it would – impossibly – imply 'it is not'. It is 'whole-limbed', present 'now', the object of thought, not of perception.[9] The Way of Doxa, introduced at the end of Fr. 8, is the way in which ordinary folk wander in ignorance, making assumptions about coming-to-be that the Way of Truth had effectively ruled out. Yet in the account offered of that second way Parmenides continues to talk, in certain contexts, of the Necessity in play. The nature, *phusis*, of the stars, for instance, is held fast within the bounds of necessity (Fr. 10), so it would clearly be incorrect to equate the contrast between truth and doxa with that between the necessary and the merely contingent.

Parmenides thus sets up a fundamental opposition between the findings of reason and those of opinion. The further step that Plato took was to construct a theory of Forms whose ontological status is radically contrasted with that of the perceptible particulars that nevertheless 'participate' in the Forms or 'imitate' them (terms that Aristotle was to criticise as mere poetic metaphor).[10] Plato's account of reality, then, allows not just for what truly or unqualifiedly is on the one hand (the *ontōs onta*), but also for what is 'in a way' (*tropon tina*), courtesy of some relationship to the truly existing and eternal Forms.[11] When he comes to offer a cosmological account, in the *Timaeus*, the contrast between the intelligible unchanging Forms and what is subject to change remains in place, though where the latter is concerned it is possible to give a 'likely account' (Burnyeat 2005) even if not a stable nor incontestable one such as he claims is possible where the Forms themselves are concerned.

It is striking that this comprehensive Platonic revision of Parmenides' fundamental ontological separation was immediately challenged and rejected by Plato's most famous, and in many respects very loyal, pupil, Aristotle. The chief respect in which Aristotle followed Plato was in endorsing the need for intelligible forms, yet their nature is now radically transformed. They continue to provide the answer to the question of the formal causes of substances or processes, that which distinguishes them from other things. The form of human being captures the essence of human beings (as

---

[9] How to understand the characteristics of Parmenides' Being and how to evaluate the arguments used to arrive at them remain among the most disputed topics in Presocratic philosophy. But all are agreed that he held that one arrives at an understanding of the Way of Truth by thinking and reasoning, not by appeals to empirical evidence.

[10] Aristotle, *Metaphysics* 991a20 ff., 1079b24 ff.

[11] *Symposium* 210e–212a. The *Phaedo* (79a) explicitly distinguishes two types of being, the visible and the invisible. At *Republic* 479cd Plato says of the many beautiful things that they also on occasion appear ugly. So the conventions of ordinary people (the many) about such matters are 'tossed about' between 'being' and 'not-being', one of many images used to describe their ambivalent ontological status.

opposed to their properties or their mere accidents) and can and should be given a clear definition. But the major departure from Plato that marks Aristotle's metaphysics is that, in the sublunary region at least, the forms do not exist independently of the things of which they are the forms. His idea of primary substance, in the *Categories* at least, is that it is the individual composite whole, consisting of form plus matter, that can be said to exist.[12] To give an account of any such individual, Socrates, say, or this olive tree, we have not only to identify its form, but also its matter, what it is made of. Indeed, for a full account we need to include two other types of cause, how the object came to be (its 'efficient cause') and its end or goal, what it is good for, what it is for it to fulfil itself, its final cause.

There are, to be sure, complications when Aristotle comes to talk of the heavens, where in any case the matter in question does not consist of the four sublunary elements and their compounds, but of the fifth element, *aithēr*.[13] But the message concerning the ordinary objects we encounter here on earth is clear. To understand them we need to give an account of their intelligible forms: but those forms do not exist independently of the compound wholes that combine matter and form. If a species were to have no living member, then it would cease to exist, though it must be stressed that Aristotle's belief in the eternity of the world rules out any possibility of such extinction events.

In later Greek philosophy and science very different views were taken on the relationship between the appearances and reality, but some recognition of the or a fundamental gap between those two is common ground to many thinkers and to many fields of inquiry. Both those points are important and I shall take some time to illustrate both.

---

[12] In the *Categories* the individual substances, Socrates, Callias, this particular horse or dog, are said to be 'primary', while their species and genera are 'secondary' substances. Elsewhere, however, in the *Metaphysics* (book Z) what is said to be primary is the essences or forms of such substances, from the point of view, in other words, of the question of what makes them the substances they are.

[13] Aristotle's doctrine of the fifth element, that is neither hot nor cold, neither wet nor dry, has often been castigated as a disaster for his and much subsequent science. It has to be granted, however, first that he thinks he has good empirical evidence – citing astronomical observations carried out by the Babylonians and Egyptians – for the conclusion that the movements of the heavenly bodies have never been subject to change (*On the Heavens* 270b13 ff., cf. 292a7 ff.). Second, once he is convinced that those movements take place perpetually – and so that must be naturally – in a circle, he argues that the heavenly bodies cannot be made of the sublunary elements, whose natural motions are either to or from the centre of the universe, identified – again in part on the basis of empirical considerations – with the centre of the spherical earth (*On the Heavens* Book 2 chs. 13–14, Book 3 ch. 2). On that account one might say that the problem was not so much that Aristotle idealised the conditions of motion in the superlunary sphere unduly, but rather that he did not abstract enough from the effects of what we would call friction and the resistence of the medium in his account of motion in the sublunary region.

In ethics, for instance, the idea that was already proposed by Plato and by Aristotle, that true pleasures are to be contrasted with merely apparent ones, continues to reverberate. Two types of mistake might be made. First you could be mistaken in your subjective impression of some pleasant experience, for such might just be illusory. But then you might need to revise your general idea of which pleasures are the most important and valuable ones. The philosophers were in business to suggest that merely transient or superficial pleasures were to be rated far lower than the true and lasting ones, which would bring you real happiness as opposed to some short-term sense of well-being.

Similarly, where friendship, for instance, is concerned, you could discover you were mistaken about the character of some person you initially took to be a friend. But again the philosophers set about contrasting different modalities of friendship, where Aristotle already distinguished between friendship based on mutual pleasure or for profit or self-interest, and the true variety based on virtue.

On the one hand, Aristotle has a healthy respect for what he calls the *endoxa*, the accepted or reputable opinions, and the 'phenomena', though that latter term can cover both what appears to the senses and what appears in the sense of what is believed to be the case. But two famous texts illustrate the ambivalences in play. At *Nicomachean Ethics* 1145b2 ff. he describes his method, and not just in ethics, as first 'positing' the 'phenomena' and after first discussing the difficulties going on to prove all the *endoxa*, or at least most of them and the most authoritative ones. Faced with the Socratic paradox that 'no one does wrong willingly' (*Nicomachean Ethics* 1145b27 f.) he says that that is in plain contradiction with the 'phenomena'.

Then in his zoology, in his convoluted discussion of the reproduction of bees, he gives us this (*On the Generation of Animals* 760b27 ff.):

> This then seems to be what happens with regard to the generation of bees, judging from theory [he means his a priori assumptions about the roles of male and female] and from what are thought to be the facts about them. However, the facts [*ta sumbainonta*: what happens] have not been sufficiently ascertained. And if they ever are ascertained, then we must trust the evidence of the senses rather than theories, and theories as well as long as their results agree with the phenomena.

So on the one hand 'what appears' is often the starting point of his own investigations and can be appealed to as evidence in arriving at his conclusions. But on the other, not all the common opinions will withstand critical scrutiny, not even all the most authoritative ones. As for the phenomena that appear to perception, some do, some do not, correspond to what careful examination reveals to be the case.

After Aristotle, in the Hellenistic period, the general epistemological doubts about the reliability of sense-perception were joined by other sceptical arguments that also undermined reason as the criterion as well. In the matter of perception, much use is made of examples of how it can be mistaken. The square tower appears round at a distance. A straight stick appears bent in water. What a healthy person perceives as sweet may taste sour to someone who is sick. Sometimes the problems relate to the circumstances of the perception, sometimes to the perceivers themselves. The positivist philosophers, Epicureans and Stoics, could agree that reports of what is perceived were liable to error, but still maintain that perception had a positive role in knowledge. The Epicurean Lucretius indeed held that all perceptions (as such) are true, while the Stoics adopted a special kind of impression, dubbed 'kataleptic', as the criterion. Meanwhile both schools invoked reason and argument, of course, to support their alternative claims concerning the underlying realities. Yet they were far from agreeing what those underlying realities consisted in, whether atoms and the void, or some adaptation of a qualitative continuum theory. Accordingly, as I noted before, the Pyrrhonian sceptics exploited such disagreements to support their view that any such search for hidden reality was doomed to failure. Those sceptics did not <u>assert</u> that there is no underlying reality at all, for to do so would be to be dogmatic. On their view, then, there was no criterion, whether perception or reason, that justified any such definite statement. Yet that left them with the recommendation that one should live by the appearances, without committing to any theories of underlying causes and realities.

One might suppose that such radical epistemological doubts and disagreements would quite undermine any efforts to engage in the empirical research of physical phenomena. Yet on the contrary, sustained inquiries in such fields as astronomy, harmonics, pneumatics, 'mechanics'[14] and medicine were carried out, culminating in the work of investigators such as Hero of Alexandria in the first century CE and Ptolemy and Galen in the second. The phenomena or perceptible appearances themselves might manifest irregularities, but some argued they could nevertheless be 'saved' by accessing the underlying realities, though this slogan of 'saving the phenomena' was, as we shall see – yet again – not unambiguous.

---

[14] On Hero of Alexandria, see Tybjerg 2004; and for a recent careful analysis of ancient Greek work in the general field of mechanics, see Berryman 2009.

The most famous example of this is in astronomical theory, where the irregularities of the apparent movements of the planets, moon and sun – the stations and retrogradations of planets, for instance – could be explained as being due to the combinations of perfectly regular circular motions, even if different views were proposed, at different periods, concerning what those circular motions themselves consisted in. Some theories postulated concentric spheres, others epicycles or eccentric circles, or – in the case of Ptolemy – combinations of both. But the upshot always was that the irregularities were merely apparent, the result of the complexity of the combination of the underlying circles. In that way those irregularities ceased to be an embarrassment for the theory and even became positive evidence *for* it. 'Saving the phenomena' could thus also be a way of saving (in this case validating) the hypotheses proposed.

So one mode of 'saving' was to reduce apparent irregularities to underlying regularities. But the actual status of the objects invoked in the models that did the explanatory work remained unclear. The idea that the models were just calculating devices that corresponded to no reality is mentioned in our ancient sources, though in certain key texts this is to express dissatisfaction with any such notion.[15] The opposing realist view, that the circles or epicycles are indeed physical realities, corresponds to the majority opinion in those practising astronomers for whom we have good concrete evidence on the point.[16] Of course the problem of determining their nature remained a major stumbling block. But astronomical theorists continued to work with such models, confident (most of them, at least) that they would eventually successfully account for the irregularities in the appearances.

A second field of investigation in which the task of 'saving the phenomena' figures is music theory.[17] The fact that the main concords of octave, fifth and fourth could be expressed in terms of the simple ratios of 2:1, 3:2 and 4:3 was known already before Plato, but different views were taken,

---

[15] The chief advocate of the so-called 'instrumentalist' view of ancient Greek astronomy was Duhem (1908), though as I endeavoured to show in Lloyd 1991: ch. 11, his interpretation of his key texts, in Proclus especially, is open to radical objections and cannot be accepted. Thus in the *Outlines* (236.15 ff.) Proclus mentions the idea that the epicycles and eccentrics are mere contrivances – that is, objects of thought – but he does so not to endorse that view (as Duhem supposed) but to reject it.

[16] As for Ptolemy himself, the second book of his treatise *Planetary Hypotheses* leaves us in no doubt that he sought a realist account of the tambourines or segments of spheres on which the planets are carried. Lloyd 1991: ch. 11, 269–71.

[17] The full story of the controversies between different musical theorists in ancient Greece is set out by Barker 1989 and 2000. In the latter book he shows how in his *Harmonics* Ptolemy very largely successfully combined the appeal to mathematical theory with perception. What a trained ear hears is both the explanandum and, when the theory has successfully done its explanation, what serves to confirm the theory.

then and later, on the question of the relation between the perceptible phenomena and the underlying mathematical relations. To those who privileged the latter, concords had to conform to one of two mathematical ratios, namely multiplicate (as in the example of 2:1 or in general n:1) or superparticular (as in 3:2 and 4:3, or in general $n+1$:n). But this meant that the interval of an octave and a fourth (expressible as the numerical ratio 8:3) cannot *be* a concord, even though to some it *sounded* like one. So once again what was perceived might be in conflict with what theory, whether arithmetical or geometrical, dictated, and at the limit the phenomena could only be 'saved' by denying what the senses reported.

It is obvious, then, that throughout Greek thought the modalities of the contrast between appearance and reality differ, even though some idea of the gap between those two is, as I put it, common ground. That gap opened up a space for the claims of rationalists of one type or another, strong ones who maintained that reason alone is to be trusted and more moderate ones who held that it was one route to knowledge, though it should be combined with sense perception and experience more generally. So my next task is to try to evaluate what elements of this binary have been shared across different cultures and which appear rather to be distinctive preoccupations of the ancient Greeks and of their legacy to later Western thought.

In a variety of contexts ancient Chinese were as alert to the possibility that the appearances are deceptive as the ancient Greeks were. One such is when problems arose in the assessment of humans' behaviour, intentions and motives. There is all the difference in the world between the true ruler and one who is king in name alone, a theme that recurs in many ancient Chinese texts (e.g. Mencius I/A 6 and 7, *Hanfeizi* 12).[18] When judging true filial piety, true courage, true goodwill, true virtue or sagehood more generally, we have to beware, for many apparent examples fail to pass muster. In the *Lüshi chunqiu* there is a chapter (22/3, *yi si*, 'spurious resemblances') that points out that distinguishing the genuine article from something that superficially resembles it is a problem not just with human character but with physical objects. The examples there are of what looks like jade but is not, and what appears to be an excellent sword but again is not.

---

[18] Mencius in the late fourth century BCE is an important source for views generally associated with Confucius. Han Fei, author of at least parts of the *Hanfeizi* in the third century BCE, is a notable critic both of those views and of those of the main early rival group of Mohists. In the *Shuo nan* chapter (12) Han Fei is also responsible for our first sustained Chinese examination of 'the difficulties of persuasion', where his focus is not so much on the logic of the argumentation used, as on the psychology of the individual whom you are trying to persuade (see Lloyd 1996a: 41).

Then a second context in which the ancient Chinese deploy a contrast between appearance and reality in ways that are strictly analogous to Greek usages relates to disease. A person may indeed appear to be healthy but in reality be sick. We find examples of this in our earliest extant Chinese medical case histories which are contained in the first great general history, the *Shiji*, composed around 90 BCE, when it sets out the biography of the second-century BCE physician Chunyu Yi. Thus case 12 relates to one of the servant girls in the palace of the King of Jibei, who did not look ill, though Chunyu Yi diagnoses an injured spleen. Even so the king himself does not think there is anything amiss, because her complexion has shown no alteration – only to be proved wrong when the girl drops dead (*Shiji* ch. 105: 2805).

It is particularly striking that one move that we find in Greece to get past the 'mere' appearances is paralleled at least up to a point also in China, namely when mathematics is invoked to get a handle on a problem. In the cosmological treatise *Zhoubi suanjing*, which I have mentioned before, the master Chenzi is questioned by his pupil Rong Fang, who says he has heard something about Chenzi's Way, namely that it is 'able to comprehend the height and size of the sun, the area illuminated by its radiance, the amount of its daily motion' and a whole range of other astronomical matters. Chenzi duly confirms that it does: 'Yes, all these things can be attained by mathematics [*suan shu*, the art or method of reckoning]', where as I have noted before (ch. 3 n. 12) one key technique is the use of gnomon shadow differences.[19] But while Chenzi says that it is possible to acquire mathematical knowledge, Rong Fang makes several failed attempts before eventually succeeding with the help of Chenzi, whose role as expert in the matter is thereby highlighted.

This shows very clearly that as in Greece so too in China we can find evidence of the idea that some understanding of the phenomena can be achieved by measuring them and by using geometry or arithmetic to bring them within reach of our understanding. Yet there may be crucial differences in the ways in which that principle is invoked and in general in how ancient authors represented the relationship between what, with important reservations, we may label 'mathematics', on the one hand, and 'physics' on the other. For their part the ancient Chinese categories *suan shu* or *shu shu*

[19] *Zhoubi suanjing* 23–4, cf. Cullen 1996: 175 ff. A second context in which Chinese theorists gave quantitative accounts of perceptible phenomena is harmonics, the analysis of musical sounds. Lloyd 2002: 56 ff. briefly sets out the main texts from *Huainanzi* and the *Shiji* and discusses the various types of approximation and idealisation that had to be entertained to get the numbers to fit the perceived harmonies.

(which we conventionally translate 'mathematics') referred to methods of reckoning or calculation, but that presupposed no ontological contrast with the things to which that calculation was applied. Of course Greek 'mathematics' is far from exactly equivalent to what we mean by that term,[20] just as their 'physics' is the study of nature more generally (Lloyd 2009: ch. 2). But in some Greek views at least there was a clear sense that mathematics deals with intelligible, not perceptible, reality, even if in some other opinions (Aristotle's most notably) the subject matter of mathematics is the mathematical properties of physical objects, not separate mathematical entities existing independently of them. We find no ancient Chinese parallel to the – Platonic – view that the reality that mathematics accesses has an altogether different ontological status from the perceptible phenomena that it explains.

The contrast between some Greek and some Chinese speculations is perhaps most interesting when dealing with overall accounts of change. Once again at a superficial level there appears to be much in common between the frequent Greek focus on the interplay of opposites and a broadly similar Chinese preoccupation. The pre-Aristotelian Pythagoreans set up a Table of Opposites, starting with Limit and the Unlimited, Odd and Even, the One and the Many, and encompassing a number of other pairs of different types, where one recurrent theme which we have discussed before is that one member of each pair carries positive overtones while the other has negative undertones. Right and left are one example, male and female another, while good and evil themselves are also included.

Now as is well known, the Chinese too appealed extensively to opposites as a basis of some account not just of physical processes but of many other things as well. Modern commentators have often drawn up Chinese tables of opposites and in many cases have some good primary evidence to justify doing so. The *Book of Changes* (*Yijing*), parts of which go back to the ninth century BCE, develops ideas connected with sixty-four hexagrams, each constituted by a combination of unbroken, *yang*, lines and broken, *yin*, ones, where the interpretation of the combinations serves as a manual of prediction and a guide to behaviour.[21] The general contrast between *yang* and *yin* is used in many other contexts, as we have seen in chapter 3

---

[20] The Greek term *mathēmatikē* from which our own 'mathematics' is derived is cognate with *mathēma* and *manthanein*, general terms for 'study' and 'to learn'. In practice when the word *mathēmatikos* is used in our texts it often refers to people engaged in 'astronomy' or 'astrology' or both.

[21] In the original version, the diviner started with bundles of sticks of yarrow or milfoil which, when they were sorted and some discarded, produced an array of six broken or unbroken lines, a hexagram. Each hexagram was accompanied with a name, a judgement, an image and commentaries on each of its constituent lines, where an added complication was that some of the lines are unstable and switch

considering Chinese cosmogonies that start from their differentiation. As a structuring principle, then, oppositions of many different types are used as commonly in China as in ancient Greece, and again as in Greece there are often hierarchical assumptions, concerning the superiority of one member of each pair to the other, in play.

However, at one point the typical Chinese view stands in marked contrast to that of the Pythagoreans. For the Chinese *yang* and *yin* are <u>interdependent</u>. You do not find *yang* devoid of *yin*, nor vice versa. When *yang* is at its height, *yin* is already beginning to re-emerge, and conversely when *yin* is at its maximum, the first signs of re-emerging *yang* appear.[22]

Standing back now and reviewing what our brief and selective cross-cultural historical study can reveal, it is clear, of course, that while distinctions and contrasts are built into any language, their modes and the assumptions made about the relationships in question manifest enormous diversity. We can here usefully bring to bear some logical distinctions that in many cases go back to Aristotle, though they do not get similar attention in the more limited extant ancient Chinese texts that deal with analogous topics. Aristotle first defined contradictories as pairs of propositions such that one must be true and the other false (*Categories* 13b2 ff., 33 ff.). Then there are contrary terms, and these come in two types: those that do, and those that do not, permit intermediates. Hot and cold and wet and dry are examples of the first group, odd and even of the second.[23] In other oppositions the contrast may be looser and may imply no difference in value nor in ontological status.

That takes us back to a fundamental point. One Greek legacy is an insistence on that radical ontological break paradigmatically exemplified by reality and appearance. That, as we have seen, can be the driving force in a search for underlying regularities, where the irregularities in the appearances can be dismissed as <u>merely</u> apparent, discarded as just so much noise.

---

into their opposite. That means that the original hexagram yields multiple possible situations, each a rich source of potential associations. The interpreters then had to apply their readings to give a verdict, e.g. of the possible success or failure of a particular enterprise, or otherwise to derive guidance as to what should be done. Shaughnessy 1997 is a reliable guide on how the *Changes* were used.

[22] See, for example, Lloyd and Sivin 2002: 198–9.

[23] Aristotle, *Categories* 12a6–8, for odd and even. For most Greeks, *arithmos*, which we conventionally translate 'number', picks out integers greater than one. Euclid (VII def. 2) defined the term as a 'multitude composed of units', and on that view one itself is not an *arithmos*. There are further complications with sub-categories of numbers termed 'even-times even', 'odd-times odd', 'odd-times even' and 'even-times odd' (e.g. Plato *Parmenides* 143e–144a), on which see Heath 1921: I, 70–3.

On the other hand, another Greek line of argument that also has its analogues in a recurrent, even dominant, Chinese set of assumptions is that we should allow interacting opposed processes equal ontological status. Both at the level of what is brought into opposition, and at that of how it can be understood, there is a potential contrast. On the one hand, we have seen Chinese notions of the interdependence of opposites in play where some Greek views would posit, as an ideal at least, the independence of one member of each pair. On the other, at the level of our understanding, the former view allows reality to be homogeneous, while the latter insists on the heterogeneity that separates reality and appearance.

Binary distinctions, the lesson is, may appear to be a homogeneous group but that is one of those appearances we should recognise to be deceptive. At one end of the spectrum there may be the idea that communication between the disjuncts is possible, at the other it is ruled out. At one end, communication, interaction, interdependence are allowed, at the other the theme is radical ontological difference and separation.

So although our study of just these two ancient societies shows that there are plenty of cross-cultural commonalities to be found, one should not miss the divergences. These are especially important where the issues are those of the ethical or evaluative implications of the underlying assumptions, and where that has consequences for claims to authority and expertise. Let me conclude with some remarks on those two points.

We have noted that in both ancient China and Greece (to go no further afield) one member of a pair of opposites is frequently given a positive value, while the other is downgraded. Male and female are one example in both those ancient societies. It is not that the Greeks were unaware of the need for both in reproduction, but true to the common assumption that ideally the superior member of the pair should and can be independent of the other, we find Aristotle, for example, claiming that in the animal kingdom it is better that male should be differentiated from female (*On the Generation of Animals*, Book 2, ch. 1, 732a1–11). In his view this separation allows the – superior – male to fulfil his – superior – potentialities. The Chinese notions of the interactions of *yang* and *yin* do not just allow for the interdependence of male and female, but also for an admixture of the feminine <u>in</u> the masculine and vice versa. Moreover, there are some famous Chinese texts that positively celebrate the feminine. In the *Daodejing* attributed to the legendary Laozi but probably compiled in the third century BCE, the recommendation is to 'know the male', but 'preserve the female' (28). 'In calm, the female overcomes the male' (61), for 'the soft and weak overcomes the stiff and strong' (36).

Yet although there are differences in the Greek and Chinese accounts of the relationship between the sexes, in reality in both these ancient societies women were, for sure, generally treated as inferior to men. So in that respect locating this contrast where it is put in tables of opposites or in views of *yin* and *yang* clearly reflects deep-seated assumptions about the social position of males and females. On that score when male is associated with the positive, female with the negative, items in those oppositions, that does not just reflect, but also supposedly confirms, those ideas about their place in society. In this and other instances what might purport to be a merely analytic distinction turns out to be heavily charged with ideological preconceptions. To set up a binary opposition and especially to emphasise the ontological contrast or the contrast in values is miles away from being a merely innocent piece of analysis even though it may present itself as such, as a straightforward description of what everyone should accept to be the case.

Another example would be the contrast between rulers and the ruled, where again the Greek ideal is that the masters should be quite independent of the slaves on whom they nevertheless – as everyone knew – depended. The master/slave opposition does not play such a key role in this domain in China, though as we have seen the contrast between ruler and minister certainly does. The more this is woven into the fabric of the story of the inherent oppositions at work in the world, the more this could be taken to corroborate the power situation with which the ancient Chinese were familiar, and the more difficult it becomes to mount any challenge to that aspect of the status quo.

So we find plenty of confirmation of what we may intuitively suspect, namely that political, ethical and social values and presumptions are in play in the focus on the importance of binary oppositions. Finally the dualist account of what is there to be known plays into the hands of, and is manipulated by, those who would lay claim to be the knowers. Those Greeks who postulated a radical ontological gap between being and seeming make more of this than the Chinese for whom there is no such fundamental gulf between their ontological statuses. The significance of the Greek position is most easily seen by observing how, in Plato, but already also in Parmenides, knowledge is correlated with what is, while mere opinion has as its subject matter what comes to be. When Being is set in fundamental opposition to Becoming or to Seeming, that underpins the contrast suggested between different levels of cognition. Of course that serves as a weapon in the hands of those who insisted on their own expertise as authorities in many different fields. The tendency to read binaries by way of association with other binaries – a tendency that I have argued is dangerously obfuscatory – is an important part of the techniques used by would-be experts to shore up their claims to that position.

No understanding is possible without making use of the distinctions which are everywhere present in every natural language. There can be no question of pronouncing all binaries to be misleading. The nub of the issue is how they are used, particularly to convey values, to enforce social distinctions and to claim superior knowledge – and that includes how modern writers continue to redeploy them (think of the continued reliance on some contrast between nature and culture). The binaries we have considered in this chapter may be particularly treacherous since they can be invoked to disenfranchise those associated with the inferior members of such pairs. But they were certainly not used in exactly the same way in ancient Greek and Chinese writers.

The Chinese certainly often speak of the difficulties of attaining correct knowledge – of the world and of how humans should behave. But they were less prone than some Greeks to try to insist that the most that could be attained in certain contexts was mere opinion. As I have argued on other occasions (Lloyd 1996a: chs. 3 and 4), they did not develop epistemological positions aiming to guarantee incontrovertible truth by way of valid argument from self-evident premises. The ideal of attaining the *Dao* was not a matter of having reasoned one's way to an understanding of it, but rather of embodying and practising it. Criticising others for false understanding, misleading advice, leading people astray, pretending to knowledge that they do not have, is common enough throughout early Chinese literature. But that was not done by way of constructing a notion of what truly is, and what indubitable knowledge consists in, which (if you accepted that notion at least) had the effect of radically downgrading most of what most people ordinarily believed, let alone of dismissing common opinions in their entirety. It is certainly the case that the Chinese sharply contrasted how people should behave with how many folk actually do, but this was less an epistemological distinction than a moral one, the contrast being one between the behaviour of the 'gentleman', *junzi*, and that of the 'petty person' (*xiao ren*) who on one ground or another fails to live up to the standard the gentleman sets.[24]

---

[24] This is a major recurrent theme in Chinese discussions of how one should behave from the *Lunyu* (*Analects*) onwards. This is a treatise that was regularly ascribed to Confucius himself, though it is now generally agreed to be a composite work, put together over an extended period by those who considered themselves his followers.

In relation to one of the contrasts we have detected, it seems possible to correlate the particular penchant that certain Greek thinkers had for the Being/Seeming dichotomy with the feature we have noticed so often before in their exchanges, namely the mode of public competitiveness that governed much of their intellectual life. Greek sages did not just let their wisdom speak for itself. They strove for pre-eminence as Masters of Truth by victory in argument. It is this rivalry that stimulates frequent appeals to second-order, epistemological, justifications which in turn often depend on and reflect ontological claims. You won the victory because your arguments were based on secure criteria for knowledge, ones that were often claimed to give access to a hidden, privileged reality beyond the grasp of ordinary people – or of your rivals. They were confined to the realm of seeming, even of mere illusion, while you could be confident in the correctness, the validity, and so the rationality, of your procedures. Or so some sought to insist.

That said, we have seen that such a feature was certainly not totally absent from ancient Chinese thought. Nor can we say that it was driven, in the Graeco-Roman world, by some characteristic of the Greek and Latin languages they spoke. We have seen evidence enough in this chapter that Chinese too could be alert in certain contexts to the contrast between what seems and what really is. The second point, the influence of language on thought, forms part of the agenda for my next chapter.

CHAPTER 5

Language, Literacy and Cognition

This chapter ventures a set of comments on a number of interconnected problems that stem, on the one hand, from the linguistic determinism and relativism associated with Sapir and Whorf, and, on the other, from Goody's thesis concerning what he called the 'domestication of the Savage Mind', where he concentrated most of his attention on the effects of the development of technologies of communication and especially of literacy. What, I aim to consider, can a careful examination of those issues tell us about how or whether rationality varies across languages or populations, and whether or to what extent literacy in particular provides the, or at least a, major stimulus to self-conscious reflections on reasoning? We shall have grounds for a very guarded set of conclusions on that score.

The Sapir–Whorf thesis has been expressed in different forms, and quite what the original proponents were committed to is rather uncertain and disputed (see Leavitt 2011). In the strongest version of the thesis, thought is determined by the language in which it is expressed; in the weaker formulations it is merely influenced by that language. In either case the influence or constraint may be construed as a matter of vocabulary or semantics, or alternatively, or in addition, of the structure or syntax of the language.

Where vocabulary is concerned, anyone who has experience of some language other than their own is bound to be familiar with terms for which there is no precise equivalent in their own mother tongue. Yet that does not mean, of course, that the ideas in question cannot be grasped nor expressed at all in that language, though their meanings will have to be conveyed by paraphrases or periphrasis, sometimes quite elaborate ones. One of my favourite examples is the Welsh term *hwyl*, used, roughly, of the inspired speech of a poet or preacher. Once you have become familiar with actual examples, you learn to recognise it with a certain amount of confidence. Yet there is always some room for doubt and disagreement about how a particular performance or performer should be judged, and further uncertainties about how this *hwyl* is to be expressed in English.

A more theoretically laden example would be the Chinese term *qi*, which has figured frequently in earlier chapters. It can be used of the breath we breathe, or the vital spirits that circulate in our bodies, or again of air in general, or of the energies at work in the physical processes around us. In one version of Chinese accounts of the origins of things (as we saw in chapter 3), cosmogony begins when the primordial *qi* starts to be differentiated. Heaven is separated from the earth, the light from the heavy, the bright from the dark and in general *yang* from *yin*. Given that to get some inkling of what is involved we have to be aware of some of the richness of the use of this term, translators frequently give up and resort to transliteration (as I have done here), rather than keep repeating the cumbersome and potentially misleading rendering as 'breath/energy' or whatever.

But as I said, when the particular natural language we first learnt lacks a particular term for a particular concept, that does not mean that no understanding of that concept is possible. As I pointed out in Lloyd 2007a: ch. 1, the existence of a particular vocabulary for colours does not determine which shades can be discriminated from which. That vocabulary may make certain distinctions salient, but experiments can be and have been conducted to assess when two shades are seen as distinct without their being *named*. That shows that such discriminability does *not* depend on the particular terminology for colours that is available in any given language or in any language whatsoever. Quite how any hue is perceived by any individual is a private matter. But we can certainly communicate something of our perception of similarities and differences in hue to others.

Two other suggestions that have been advanced, including by some of the most distinguished sinologists (Graham, for instance), relate first to the peculiar characteristics of the Greek verb 'to be' and second to grammatical differences in parts of speech not just in Greek but in Indo-European languages more generally. The first relates to the particular range of uses that the verb *einai* possesses (Kahn 1973), not just predicative, identitative and locative but also existential, when the verb can be used absolutely to signify what exists. Yet that feature of the verb does nothing to explain the understandings of Being that different Greek thinkers entertained, which exhibit in any case very great diversity, as we saw in the last chapter. That diversity owes nothing to the behaviour of a verb that was common to all the thinkers in question. Nor, in my opinion, can that feature be invoked to distinguish Greek ideas from Chinese ones in this area, even though, to express the idea of existence, the Chinese do not use a verb with the same range as *einai*. Thus the term *you* ('there is', 'have') serves perfectly well in many contexts to indicate what exists.

Then the argument correlating parts of speech with Greek or Indo-European categories may look superficially attractive. Substance looks as if it may reflect the prominence of substantives, while qualities correspond to adjectives, and action and being acted upon to verbs in the active or passive voice. Yet first, not all Aristotelian categories directly reflect a specific grammatical form. Place, position and state (which he exemplified with 'in the market', 'sits' and 'has shoes on' respectively) do not do so straightforwardly. Second, a quite different theory of categories was proposed by the Stoics, who suggested a division between (1) substrates, (2) the qualified, (3) the disposed and (4) the relatively disposed (e.g. Simplicius, *On Aristotle's Categories* 66.32 ff., Long and Sedley 1987: 27F, 163). Third, when the Chinese came to translate Aristotle's ideas in the seventeenth century, they found no insuperable difficulty in doing so (Wardy 2000). True, they had to use paraphrases and suggest different meanings for existing terms. But then so also had the Latin translators of his texts – and it was of course their Latin renderings of those texts that the Chinese translators themselves were using. Aristotle himself, let us recall, had to coin new expressions in his metaphysics, notably the phrase *to ti ēn einai*, for 'essence', a word we derive from Latin *essentia*, itself one of the coinages introduced by Roman writers in connection with their rendering of Greek philosophy.

But what about the differences that different syntactic structures may introduce and the barriers that they might be thought to imply to mutual intelligibility? As I have pointed out before (Lloyd 2014: 117), it was at one time claimed that ancient Chinese does not allow for the expression of counterfactual conditionals (Bloom 1981). That notion did not take long to be exposed as an extravagant mistake. Not only do ancient Chinese texts offer plenty of examples where counter-to-fact situations are contemplated: there is even a particular phrase that marks them out. This is *jia shi*, where the *shi* corresponds to 'if', but the *jia* that qualifies it stands for 'falsely', so the phrase as a whole can be rendered 'falsely supposing' (cf. Harbsmeier 1998: 116 ff.).

It is clear that this diagnosis of a systematic weakness in the ancient Chinese language owed more to the prejudices or narrow-minded expectations of those who proposed the idea than to the characteristics of that language[1] – and the same may be said of the common charge that

---

[1] In the early days of the development of comparative linguistics the idea that languages could be judged superior or inferior depending on how closely they conformed to some ideal (usually identified with Sanskrit) was common. Wilhelm von Humboldt's study of the diversity of human language structure (originally 1836), for example, expressed such a view in no uncertain terms (see Humboldt 1988).

Chinese is inherently hopelessly ambiguous. Ambiguity is a feature of every natural language: it can be exploited, indeed deliberately, including for the purposes of deception; but it can also be avoided. It is a common feature of Chinese rhetoric and diplomacy that the position one speaker adopts is left open-ended at the outset, and the partners in conversation try to turn that to their advantage in subsequent exchanges. But we should not suppose that the ancient Chinese were any different from anyone else in being perfectly capable of saying exactly what they wanted to say, and with the degree of clarity and precision they thought appropriate to the particular context. That is true even when the point they are conveying is how difficult it is to express profound meanings adequately.

At the same time we cannot fail to observe that there are differences between different natural languages in the ease with which certain complex relations can be expressed. Unlike Chinese, the highly inflected Greek and Latin languages deploy a whole battery of different grammatical structures to convey different modalities of conditionals. Once again, however, it would be a mistake to conclude from the fact that there are differences in the syntactic structures available that these languages are mutually unintelligible or that they reflect different degrees of 'rationality' – whatever that might mean in context. Translation is always difficult and for sure is never perfect. Conveying what we hope to be more or less the 'same' thought in different forms of expression in the <u>same</u> natural language will always introduce some slight modification,[2] and that is even before we factor in the pragmatics of the communication situation, the body language of the speakers, or the relationships between them. Even when exactly the same words are repeated, the very fact that on the second or subsequent occasions we are dealing with a repetition alters their force.

The analyses of Sapir and Whorf remain valuable where they serve as reminders that the interpretation of any speech act or piece of writing always presents a formidable challenge, calling for the greatest sensitivity to the nuances of vocabulary, to the subtleties of syntax, to the consequences of the point that McLuhan insisted upon, that the medium is the message. But we can and should resist any conclusion to the effect that translation cannot even get off the ground since it is always blocked at the outset, let alone any further conclusion that our thoughts are

---

[2] What precisely are the conditions of identity where thought is concerned? For certain purposes we may treat the meanings of statements in isolation from the contexts of communication in which they occur. But that is an idealisation. Once pragmatic considerations are taken into account, the problem of identity turns into something of a chimera. As Skinner (1966, 1969, 1975) and Dunn (1968) pointed out long ago, it is not ideas that can properly be said to have a history, only individuals thinking them.

hopelessly constrained by the particular natural language in which we express them.

No more should we suppose that the differences between scientific paradigms to which Kuhn (1970) drew attention present insurmountable barriers to mutual comprehension. Even when the key terms used undergo dramatic shifts in sense and reference, their transformations can be plotted – as Kuhn himself amply demonstrated in practice. We shall, in the process, have to adjust many of our starting assumptions and revise our previous understandings as we come to terms with the new paradigm. True, there is no strictly neutral vocabulary into which different paradigms can be parsed: but then no vocabulary whatsoever is totally neutral. Learning at the frontiers of science is no different in principle from the learning we were involved in from the moment we were born. True, as we advance in understanding we shall also need to unlearn what we thought we had securely grasped. But that too is an experience that starts in infancy.

My debunking of certain suggestions concerning the barriers between languages should not be taken to imply that I simply flatly refuse to recognise that skills in language use vary across individuals and groups. Quite the contrary. What can be conveyed by a master craftsman in poetry or in prose never ceases to amaze. We come back to such writings again and again and discover more and more in them, concluding often, indeed, that their meanings are practically inexhaustible. But I come back to the essential point for my argument, that is that though understanding is never perfect, some understanding is never impossible. Even when someone reports an entirely personal, subjective experience, and protests that he or she is unable to describe that at all adequately, the listener will grasp that <u>some</u> experience is being conveyed, however <u>inadequately</u> that may be, and will make the most of such clues as the report may suggest. I shall return to that point in the next chapter.

The reference, just now, to high literature takes me to my second main theme, that of the difference that literacy may make; though, to be sure, predominantly oral groups have often had supreme poets. However, the topic of the relevance of literacy and of technologies of communication in general was opened up by Goody in his pioneering *The Domestication of the Savage Mind* (1977), which accordingly merits particular attention here. Goody took as his starting-point Lévi-Strauss's discussion of *La Pensée sauvage*, somewhat misleadingly translated as *The Savage Mind* (Lévi-Strauss 1966), and he made plain at the outset how dissatisfied he was with the standard dichotomies 'advanced' and 'primitive', 'open' and 'closed', 'domesticated' and 'savage', 'hot' and 'cold' and so on, that had been much used in discussing supposed varieties in cognitive faculties and sometimes indeed in rationality.

So Goody insisted that his was no Great Divide theory. On the contrary, his focusing on the technologies of communication allowed for a more nuanced and gradational account of the broad sweep of human cognitive development. Two of his key arguments concern (a) the consequences of literacy (where he was clear that this is a matter of degree, not an all-or-nothing contrast) and (b) the differences that different modalities in the writing system can make, in brief the advantages of an alphabetic script.[3]

But although he ended up with a position that contrasted starkly with the crudest forms of the binaries in Lévi-Strauss and elsewhere, 'science of the concrete' versus 'science of the abstract', and the like, Goody still stuck with the notion of a savage mind, out there, as his title puts it, to be 'domesticated'. He had no truck with what he called the 'diffuse relativism' that 'refuses to recognise long-term differences and regards each "culture" as a thing on its own, a law unto itself' (Goody 1977: 151), even though there is a certain hesitancy in his parting shot at the end of the book. Having spoken of different kinds of problem-raising and problem-solving and the role of lists, the formula and the table, he ended (Goody 1977: 162), 'if we wish to speak of the "savage mind", these were some of the instruments of its domestication'. His may be said to be a Grand Transition theory, then, even if not a Great Divide one.

The debate that this study generated has moved on in the intervening four decades, in three areas in particular. First there has been a good deal of fruitful work on the tricky problem of the relative ease of the acquisition of different scripts.[4] Japan provides, of course, a notable test case, since Japanese children are first taught *kana* (a syllabary) before they move on to learn *kanji*, which is an adaptation of Chinese graphs. The consensus is that *kana* are easier to learn, though that advantage, at an early stage, has not led (as some might have thought it might have led) to the atrophy of *kanji*. This might be thought to be relevant to the theses of Sapir and Whorf and their associates that I have just been discussing. Yet it does nothing to show that language, however spoken or written, constrains thought. The most it might suggest is the difference in the relative speeds with which learn-ing to write a language occurs using different scripts to represent it. The contrast between learning either form of written Japanese and learning an

---

[3] These remain important themes even in later works by Goody that modified some of the arguments of Goody 1977, e.g. Goody 1986 and 1987.

[4] See, for example, Rozin, Poritsky and Sotsky 1971; Sakamoto and Makita 1973; Taylor and Taylor 1983; Kennedy 1984; Rayner and Pollatsek 1989; Olson and Torrance 1991; and Olson 1994.

alphabetic script is another matter, on which diverging opinions continue to be expressed. However, we may agree that once the Chinese invention of printing with movable type came to Europe, the limited number of characters in the alphabet (compared with the great variety of Chinese graphs) must undoubtedly have facilitated a more rapid dissemination of printed texts.

Then a second area where investigations have moved on relates to that last point and concerns the different modalities of the recording of ideas, picking up the close attention that Goody paid to aides-memoire of different types. The ways in which pictorial representations can serve as records has been studied by Severi (2015) in particular, drawing on a wealth of earlier indigenous American ethnography. Goody's claim was that literacy facilitates recording, and once records are available, this may stimulate the development of criticism and scepticism, challenges to traditional beliefs and so increased possibilities for innovation.

But apart from registering that written records in non-alphabetic scripts antedate alphabetic ones by centuries, we should now take into account that pictures may convey and preserve information of many different kinds. So one might observe that it is not so much the availability of records that is important, as the ways in which not just records but memories more generally are accessed and redeployed by different groups. It is evident that what any given group assumes about the past and its relationship to the present may make a very great difference, their notion of history, for instance, if indeed they have some sense of moving on from a past to a different present. That assumption is far from universal, for Humphrey and Hürelbaatar (2013), for example, have shown how, for the Mongols they studied, the past is still very much present.[5] I would conclude that in this case – we shall see there are others – it is not so much the material characteristics of the techniques of communication that are important as the surrounding assumptions made about what is communicated and the contexts in which that occurs.

To corroborate that suggestion I may turn back to a point that has been raised in criticism of one aspect of Goody's thesis, namely the ways in which records can be used. Goody himself already drew attention to what may happen in situations of restricted literacy – such as has been the norm everywhere around the world until very modern times. Members of the

---

[5] They draw attention to the implications of the fact that, unlike ourselves when we consider the past as 'behind' us, the Mongols they studied refer to the past as 'in front' of them. As remarked before, an interest in recording the past ('historiography') takes different forms in different ancient and modern societies.

literate elite may use writing helpfully to transmit information to one another and across time, but the content of texts is communicated by literates to non-literates in ways that reflect the imbalance between them. In these circumstances it is often the case, as Goody wrote, that 'the scribal culture continues, the *literati* hold onto their monopoly, the mandarinate maintains control' (Goody 1977: 151–2).

These points were taken up and considerably amplified in criticism of Goody by Jonathan Parry (1985) in his discussion of the effects of literacy in Indian societies. So far from the end result of increasing literacy being to foster criticism and scepticism, it may be anything but that. Rather, this technology may be used to perpetuate the privileged position of the ruling elite. Once a text achieves the status of a canon, let alone that of a sacred text conveying the words of God, criticism becomes increasingly difficult, even dangerous. The status of canonical texts in different cultures needs much further study, but certainly such texts are a phenomenon exhibited across pretty well all highly literate cultures, with similarly mixed results in each. They ensure that those canons will be preserved, but also usually inhibit challenges to their authority.

In both ancient China and ancient Greece there is ample evidence of the dual character of the consequences of literacy. In China certain canons got to form the curriculum of the Imperial Academy founded by Han Wu Di (Nylan 2001). There were paid positions for those who taught their contents (though those were far from all standardised). However, by that very fact those who sought to hand down other learning found it difficult to do so and tended to be marginalised. The institutionalising of what we may call higher education was a two-edged sword, helping to guarantee the transmission of particular works, though excluding others, including especially those that offered a very different message from the canons. While the works of Mozi were prominent in the Warring States period, when they were perceived as the main rival to the writings associated with Confucius, after the unification of China in the Qin and Han dynasties much less attention came to be paid to what passed as Mozi's teaching. At points, indeed, that teaching was all but eclipsed.

We find analogous phenomena in ancient Greece, though we may start with one important point of difference, namely that in the Graeco-Roman world there was no equivalent to the Chinese Imperial Academy with its state-sanctioned curriculum. Rather, higher learning was carried out in private institutions such as Plato's Academy, Aristotle's Lyceum, the Stoa and Epicurus' Garden. No one school in philosophy held a monopoly. But the points of similarity with the Chinese experience include the way in which the construction of self-proclaimed elites led to the marginalisation of those who did not belong. This was particularly the case where those thus marginalised did not communicate what they knew in writing in the first place.

The evidence for Greek medicine provides a particularly striking example.[6] The so-called Hippocratic treatises are a very heterogeneous lot, though the authors represented were all by definition literate and can be said to have belonged to a medical elite, even though no ancient Greek doctor could justify his right to practise medicine by invoking legally recognised qualifications. This was for the simple reason that there was no ancient equivalent for that modern phenomenon. However, we know of quite a number of other types of healer already in the fifth and fourth centuries, although the evidence for their ideas and practices is generally indirect. Thus there were important groups of women healers, labelled *maiai* (conventionally translated 'midwives', though it is clear that they were not just involved in obstetrics and what we call gynaecology). Then we hear of those called 'root-cutters' who collected materia medica in the fields and forests, and 'drug-sellers' who sold them in the markets.

Then a more impressive and successful group were those who practised medicine in the shrines of Asclepius and other healing gods and heroes. They in turn may be distinguished from the 'purifiers' who are famously attacked for their charlatanry in the treatise *On the Sacred Disease* and who are described by Plato as selling charms and incantations door-to-door, in other words without the backing of well-established religious shrines (*Republic* 364bc; cf. *Laws* 909a–d). In the great majority of such cases we depend on what we hear about their practices from the critical remarks we find in authors who themselves belonged to the elite, and given that the doctors among them were intent on securing their own reputations and undermining those of rivals, they were certainly far from unbiased witnesses.

Thus a group of writings by anonymous authors was first collected together by Alexandrian scholars and associated with Hippocrates, even though doubts about the authenticity of some of these texts begin at the same time. Certainly the internal contradictions within the Hippocratic

---

[6] Early Chinese medicine offers certain parallels. Before the medical canon, *Huangdi neijing*, came to occupy a position of dominance, around the turn of the millennium, we hear of other traditions of medical practice. The evidence from excavated tombs, dating from the second century BCE at Mawangdui and other sites, shows that some such practitioners were literate, though we can only guess how widespread the circulation of their texts was (see Harper 1998). The doctor Chunyu Yi, also from the second century BCE, was himself a member of the elite, but he too refers to a variety of other healers, both named and unnamed, including some he calls 'ordinary' doctors (see Hsu 2010).

Corpus suggested that not all could have been by a single author, and so the hunt was on to establish which were the genuine works of the historical figure, Hippocrates, who had been represented as a skilled and famous doctor already by Plato and Aristotle. But given that much later, in the second century CE, Galen was to take Hippocrates himself (as he reinterpreted him) as the 'guide to all that is good', that ensured that certain works were not just preserved but treated as authoritative. Galen himself set about drawing up a programme for the basic education of doctors, starting with some of his own works, several of which have the fact that they were addressed 'to Beginners' in their titles.

A second Greek example of this process of the canonisation of certain works and the consequent exclusion of others is, of course, mathematics. Once Euclid's *Elements* came to be generally accepted as a compendium of basic mathematical learning, that fact tended to eclipse the work of most of his predecessors. And a third example is astronomy, where Ptolemy's *Syntaxis* led to a similar overshadowing of the work of many earlier astronomers, even all but one of the treatises written by the evidently highly original Hipparchus.

As these instances show, the negative effects of the dominance of a particular group of writings were widespread, on their rivals among other texts as well as and more especially on the views of those who left no writings at all. At the same time, that dominance ensured the preservation and transmission of what the elite chose to present as the essentials of the subject. Their texts were indeed closely scrutinised and made the subject of countless commentaries. The extent to which those commentaries criticised the contents of the canonical writings varied. In general the stated aim of the commentators was indeed to preserve earlier knowledge, not to attempt to go beyond it with innovations and criticisms.[7] Even when we can see new ideas being brought into play (as notably in some of the late Aristotelian commentators),[8] they are sometimes not hailed as such, but represented as already contained implicitly in the canonical writings themselves.

---

[7] A notable case of a Chinese commentator who represents himself as essentially preserving the teaching in the canonical *Book of Changes*, but who certainly elaborates its doctrines and goes far beyond them, is Yang Xiong, active around the turn of the millennium (see Nylan and Sivin 1995).

[8] In the sixth century CE, Simplicius and Philoponus both introduced new ideas in the discussion of what we would call dynamical problems, Simplicius generally representing himself as faithful to Aristotelian views while Philoponus challenged them. Famously Philoponus referred to what he claimed as empirical evidence to show that the speed of a falling body does not vary directly with its weight. In this context he introduces an idea of impetus that had far-reaching implications for later discussions of the topic. See, for example, Sambursky 1962.

We should conclude at this point, therefore, that while Goody was certainly correct to point out that increasing literacy could facilitate the development of criticism and scepticism, we have to recognise that that was far from always its result, for in many fields the existence of canonical texts inhibited innovation. Nor should we imagine, conversely, that those critical and sceptical tendencies were generally lacking in predominantly oral societies. There is a wealth of ethnographic evidence to the point. It may be that criticism of those who purported to have special knowledge, shamans, for instance, was more generally directed at individuals, rather than at the basis for any such claim – that is to say at the very possibility of shamanic knowledge in the first place. But even there we can find potential exceptions. The story of the Kwakiutl Quesalid illustrates this.[9] He is reported as having started out on his career by doubting the claims not just of this or that individual shaman, but of shamans in general. So he set out to learn what he considered their tricks of the trade. Yet the effect of his mastering these was the reverse of what he had expected. For instead of his fellow Kwakiutl coming to the conclusion that this was all trickery and deceit, they thought of him as not just an ordinary shaman but a quite superior one.

The cognitive effects of transformations in the technology of communication have obviously been – and continue to be – complex. Some of the strongest elements in Goody's argument relate to the material support available. The modern use of computers has, of course, had profound repercussions on the ways in which complex data may be stored and accessed, offering the possibility of new styles of manipulation and modelling. But ancient examples to illustrate the general point can also be given. In a now classic study of the use of lettered diagrams in Greek geometry, Netz (1999) showed just what the reasoning owed to them. There are two points here. First, the investigation of complex geometrical properties is hardly conceivable without reference to some visual representation. Then, second, the way the diagram is built up, by identifying points in a sequence that generally follows that of the Greek alphabet, alpha, beta, gamma and so on, is crucial to the construction of the proof. The construction of the diagram is indeed the construction of the proof, and the Greek term *diagramma* can be used of both.[10]

---

[9] Quesalid's story was reported by Boas 1930 and then taken up in Lévi-Strauss 1968 [1958]: 175 ff.

[10] While the ancient Chinese did not put the diagram to use in Greek-style deductive demonstrations in geometry, there are plenty of instances where their reasoning too depended on visual representations. I mentioned the diagrams in the *Book of Changes* in the last chapter and many other examples of the role of charts, maps and images are discussed in Bray, Dorofeeva-Lichtmann and Métailié 2007.

So far as other aspects of Goody's thesis go, we can agree that once literacy is widespread, there is less need to memorise what passes as knowledge, whether in the form of oral or of written instruction, though when we learn a practical skill, that may owe little to what is expressible in words, much more to repeated practice itself.[11] Nowadays where texts are concerned we generally do not have to master, let alone commit to memory, the primary ones, nor even the literature on them. We just have to have the minimum skills of knowing how to access them online. That undoubtedly frees up a lot of cognitive capacity. Whether that is then devoted to criticism and to innovation is another matter. Their flourishing will depend on the structure of interpersonal relations, the acceptance of the value of debate and dissent, for instance, as much as on anything else.

Thus Great Divide theories, about which Goody himself was sceptical, may obfuscate some of the issues. At least the effects of literacy in its different modes are ambivalent. The experience of ancient societies, insofar as we can reconstruct it, hardly confirms any radical thesis of a fundamental cognitive transformation brought about by the spread of literacy. There may, to be sure, be a growth of self-awareness in the techniques of interpersonal communication, in those of persuasion, for instance. Once certain features of argument had been identified as such, they could be appealed to in order to score positive or negative points. With a vocabulary to identify flaws in argument – such as inconsistency, circular reasoning, begging the question, ambiguity – you could bring that to bear against opponents. They had then either to claim that they had not committed the fault or that it was no fault at all, entering thereby into a second-order discussion of the modalities of reasoning.

However, the crucial qualification that needs to be entered is that the development of a certain self-consciousness about argument does not require literacy. Gluckman's studies of the Barotse provided abundant evidence to the point (Gluckman 1965, 1967, 1972), for while at the time he reported on them they were a basically non-literate society, they not only nevertheless prided themselves on their considerable skills in rhetoric and their connoisseurship in the matter, but also had an extensive vocabulary to refer to the virtues and vices that different speakers exhibited.

---

[11] Both Greek and Chinese authors make the point that book learning by itself is not enough to acquire certain practical skills. Aristotle does so in relation to medicine, for instance (*Nicomachean Ethics* 1181b2–3), and *Zhuangzi* with regard to many of the crafts those texts celebrate (as cited in ch. 3 n. 18). Thus in *Zhuangzi* 13 the carpenter Bian says he is unable to explain even to his son how to use his chisel (the story is repeated in *Huainanzi* 12, 9b–10a).

The existence of explicit categories of second-order characteristics of reasoning can certainly facilitate certain argumentative moves, as I argued already in Lloyd 1990. Chinese rhetoric exemplifies this, when accusations of inconsistency were made, for instance. Greek discussion of the possible flaws in reasoning is a good deal richer. In his *Sophistical Refutations* (chs. 3–15) Aristotle identified more than a dozen modes of fallacy, some dependent on diction or language, others not. He aimed to equip his readers with the skills needed in their engagement in the extensive actual debates held in so many different contexts in classical Greek city-states. At the same time we must not lose sight of the obvious point that being able to diagnose a fallacy did not mean an end to fallacious reasoning: having a second-order vocabulary to identify weaknesses in argument did not make those weaknesses disappear. Such transformations that occurred were a question of the degree of explicitness possible about the characteristics of argumentative moves, not a matter of any radical changes in the correctness of the conduct of argument itself.

Where both ancient and modern societies are concerned, the key question relates to what stimulates the development of such explicit reflections on the nature of reasoning. If the growth of literacy by itself cannot provide the answer, then we must look elsewhere for relevant factors. We should start, to be sure, by asking in what contexts discussion and debate are practised, and again the variety across both literate and non-literate societies is considerable. Yet this is no more than what we should expect, given that the norm will be for those debates to be conducted in the oral mode.

While, as usual, generalisation is hazardous, some differences in the key modalities and contexts of communicative exchange do stand out. In ancient India (as we can see from the *Upaniṣads*, for instance (cf. Lloyd 2014: ch. 2)) it is the gurus themselves who decide who has won the argument.[12] The victor is the guru who quite literally has the last word, having asked a question that none of the others can answer: you are supposed not to ask questions to which you do not know the answer yourself and the issues under discussion can indeed be very abstruse, to do with the nature of Brahman or the number of gods there are, for instance. What was at stake was reputation, though in some debates, held in the courts of kings, the aim was less reaching the truth than entertaining the courtiers.

---

[12] Among the many critical studies of the development of argument and debate in ancient India, see especially Matilal 1985, 1998; Mohanty 1992; Prets 2000, 2001; and Bronkhorst 2002, 2007.

In China many philosophical controversies were conducted in writing and with long-dead opponents. Being disputatious (for which the term was *bian*[1]) was frowned on, as many Warring States texts confirm.[13] But discussion (*lun*) was acceptable, though that might be more a matter of explaining a point of view than of arguing. However, we also have evidence of live debates not just (most frequently) on matters of policy, but also on astronomical and calendrical issues, held not just among the learned in private, but sometimes very much in public, in courts or palaces before officials or ministers who represented the king or (after the unification) the emperor (see Cullen 2007). But there the debaters themselves did not generally decide the outcome, which was ultimately in the hands of the officials or the ruler himself. What was at stake was not just some set of abstract, theoretical issues, but ones that had deep implications for the state; that is, for good governance.

We find some of the same patterns and circumstances in Greece. There too there were debates in the courts of rulers (kings, tyrants) where sometimes the aim was rather entertainment than edification. But one rather distinctive Greek custom was to hold open debates in which the decision was taken neither by the debaters nor by some official in charge but by the audience itself, whether by acclaim or by voting, sometimes indeed by secret ballot.

There were three main contexts in which this occurred – politics (in the assemblies that in many Greek city-states were plenipotentiary), the law and what we may call specialist or higher education. Thus in the political assemblies, policy issues, not just decisions on particular affairs but even on the constitution itself, were voted on by the citizen body as a whole.

Second, in the law courts, both verdicts of guilt or innocence, and sentences, were decided by bodies of 'dicasts' (as they were called) who combined the roles of judge and jury. There were, in other words, no separate, let alone professionally qualified, judges. In Athens these dicasts could number up to 5,001 – though that was rare. But a body numbering in the hundreds was normal (there were 501 dicasts at Socrates' trial). And the Athenians devised elaborate systems not just to ensure that particular jurors were chosen for particular trials at random, but also that the voting procedures were by secret ballot.

Third, there were the debates held by travelling lecturers ('sophists') who put on rival showpiece speeches (they were called *epideixeis*) on any subject

---

[13] See, for example, Mencius 3B/9; cf. *Zhuangzi* 33: 30, 74, 79, 86. Graham (1989: 167 ff.) has argued for a positive valence for *bian*[1] as argumentation among the Mohists, but this is in a sense that is related to its homophone *bian*[2], where the basic meaning is 'distinguish' or 'discriminate'.

that they thought people would pay to hear them discuss.[14] These included not only such topics as grammar, but also astronomy and element theory, and the constitution of the human body or the causes of diseases. It is remarkable that the winner in some such debates was decided by the lay audience, as was the case in the disputes on the physical constitution of the human body that are mentioned in the Hippocratic treatise *On the Nature of Man* – a point that underlines the fact that the gap between layperson and self-styled expert was far smaller than we are used to. How serious were such performances? The answer varies, but the point to bear in mind is that one of the objects of the exercise from the sophists' own point of view was to impress members of the audience so that they would sign up for the more extended lecture courses that the sophists also offered for those who were prepared to pay for them. These exhibitions were indeed publicity for those who put them on.

Rather than the mere facts of literacy or of the particular alphabetic script favoured in Greece, it is these contexts of communicative exchange that provide the key to a better understanding of the development of new styles of argument, to that aspect of cognitive practice at least. The best illustration of this point comes if we consider the negative reaction that common modes of persuasion provoked first in Plato, then in Aristotle and subsequently more widely afield. One might have imagined that the consensus among ancient Greeks would be that the best way to decide on most issues would be to take a vote and see what the majority held. But that was emphatically not the view that Plato and Aristotle took.

Plato represents his great hero Socrates as being profoundly dissatisfied with the types of argument that were common not just in political and legal life but across the intellectual spectrum. The audiences present at such debates could not be relied on to make correct judgements about policy issues, about legal ones, or indeed about any technical subject whatsoever. What was needed – it was thought – was experts who could produce not merely persuasive arguments, but demonstrative ones. For that, Socrates and Plato demanded clear definitions to start with, and truths that were applicable right across the domain under discussion. Plato did not set out one ideal method of proof, but as we have remarked, Aristotle certainly did, laying down the conditions that had to be met, namely self-evident primary

---

[14] Greek sophists shared with Chinese 'wandering persuaders' of the Warring States period that they moved from one state to another, but their typical audiences were very different. Chinese persuaders generally targeted rulers or those in government, while Greek sophists taught a wide range of subjects to anyone who was prepared to pay their fees.

premises and valid arguments. Thus was created a notion of axiomatic–deductive demonstration that was able to deliver incontrovertible conclusions – provided both conditions were fulfilled. Once that ideal existed, it became, in Greece, the goal that not just some mathematicians and logicians set themselves, but even theologians such as Proclus and doctors such as Galen. But if the ambition for certainty was clear, the difficulties of meeting the conditions for attaining it, especially securing those self-evident primary premises, were often underestimated. Here was a formidable tool that offered the prospects of indisputable results and knock-down arguments over opponents – except that the possibility of challenging the premises always remained. On the one hand, we can register how techniques of argument developed and were made explicit. On the other, we have to remark that in certain respects the new ideal had constraining, rather than liberating, effects when the demand was for ungainsayability.

This provides, then, a striking example of the development of a brand-new ideal for demonstration, one that was unique to ancient Greece among ancient civilisations. So here we have an instance of one type of domestication, one that depended on making certain rules explicit. But if we ask what that development owed to literacy, we can see the qualifications that need to be entered to that part of Goody's thesis.

Of course, in a sense the ways in which Plato and Aristotle criticised the rhetoric practised by their contemporaries illustrate the importance of there being some room for manoeuvre to criticise traditional beliefs and practices from within the society that prized them. But the particular criticism they mounted, and more importantly the ideal that Aristotle set up to replace the existing patterns of debate, owe nothing to a specific mode of (alphabetic) literacy and not much, I would say, even to literacy levels as a whole. To be sure, the audiences of the debates in each of the three contexts I identified were citizens of the various city-states who were expected to be minimally literate, but the addition of 'minimally' is crucial.[15] Many could do no more than write their own names, despite the fact that laws and edicts were regularly inscribed on tablets and set up in public places so that any citizen who could read had access to them. If one goes along with the arguments for the superiority of the alphabetic script to its rivals in promoting literacy (despite the reservations that may be expressed on that score), then one could say that the development of the political institutions of Athens was helped by the existence of that basic pool of minimally

---

[15] The extent of Athenian literacy in the fifth and fourth centuries BCE remains a hotly disputed topic. Rosalind Thomas 1989 provides a salutary corrective to the over-optimistic Havelock 1982, 1986.

literate citizens.[16] But that does not negate what is to my mind the more important point that this was still very much a face-to-face society, confrontational indeed, where it was skills in speaking in public that counted, certainly far more than general literacy and far more than the fact that there were those written texts that could be consulted by those with that skill – and then pondered critically, as Goody would have it.

So if we focus on just this one aspect of a certain 'domestication' for the moment, what can we say? For one important transition in the ways in which argument was conducted for which we have good concrete evidence from ancient societies, the crucial factors seem to lie in the circumstances in which communicative exchange was practised, who participated, what the rules of engagement were, who decided those and how claims to superior knowledge and prestige were mounted and validated. Alongside the argument from changes in the technologies of communication we need to add in more general, social, cultural and political considerations, complex as these are liable to be. Evidently no simple correlation can be established between political regimes and dissent. It was not just autocratic rulers who wiped out their opponents, although they may have done so more ruthlessly and systematically than democratic regimes (I shall be mentioning Socrates again in chapter 6). However, it was not just democratic Athens that prided itself on free speech, *parrhēsia*. As Schaberg (1997) and others (cf. Lloyd 2005) have shown, Chinese persuaders in the Warring States and Qin and Han periods were recognised to have a duty to remonstrate with their rulers when they saw them adopting policies that went against the interests of the state and of good government more generally. Not only did they have such a duty, but many of them fulfilled it, even at the cost of losing their position and not infrequently even their lives. The tactics that you needed to employ to make your criticisms heard varied with the circumstances, but both ancient civilisations cultivated the skills needed to a high degree.

We return, then, to the argument I proposed in chapter 2, that different manifestations of thought and reasoning should not lead us to conclude that different human populations differ in that some have, but others lack, certain cognitive capacities themselves. Those manifestations reflect the different opportunities for their expression, which in turn for sure depend on the social and political circumstances that obtain, the values that are

---

[16] In the Athenian institution of ostracism, citizens wrote down the name of the politician they wanted to exile from the state on a sherd (*ostrakon*). But a hoard of pre-prepared sherds all naming Themistocles in the same hand (or a very limited number of them) shows that not all citizens did the writing down themselves; cf. Vanderpool 1970.

held in esteem, the roles of individuals or groups who laid some claim to intellectual or moral leadership, and the extent to which they articulated the ideals for which they stood. But thus far there are no grounds to hold that humans differ in the cognitive equipment they possess. We have, however, yet to consider a range of contexts in which a diagnosis of irrationality may at first sight seem not just obvious but inevitable. My next chapter will be devoted to the challenge that some such beliefs and practices present.

CHAPTER 6

Gods, Spirits, Demons, Ghosts, Mysticism, Miracles, Magic, Myth

The heterogeneous items picked out in the title of this chapter all represent examples where we may have every reason to feel at a loss. How can we begin to explain what is involved in the belief that such entities or experiences exist? How can we understand the origins and importance of such ideas? The further major problem that such a list presents is whether or to what extent we can generalise across very diverse views and practices across different societies, whether contemporary or accessed through the historical record.

Let me venture some preliminary elaborations of those points. Although some may think that it is relatively straightforward to identify what counts as a 'god' in any given culture, in practice the items that are so identified present a bewildering heterogeneity, as do the related experiences of the divine, as James (1902) showed so brilliantly. Some gods are anthropomorphic, though if they take the shape of humans, they are very different from humans by virtue of their immortality and indestructibility. Some may take the form of other animals, and many more resemble no other living beings at all. The example of Buddhism poses the question whether it is necessarily the case that any religion must imply a concept of God, as opposed, rather, just to some notions of the holy, the numinous, the spiritual.

In many systems of belief and ritual practice there is something of a hierarchy, between higher and lesser divine beings, though the boundaries between such may be fuzzy, unstable and permeable. On death, individuals may become ghosts or spirits, maybe dangerous ones, demons indeed, until such time as the proper rituals have been performed, as Sterckx (2002) and Puett (2002 and forthcoming) have discussed for ancient China, for instance. In ancient Greece, too, we find quite a variety of beliefs expressed on what survives death. In Homer, once the person has received due burial rites, the *psuchē* has a tenuous existence as a wraith in Hades. In some of the philosophers (the Pythagoreans, Empedocles) there is the belief that on death the person is reborn, in some kind of life-form, not necessarily a human, indeed not necessarily an animal, depending on how they have lived their lives. That view is echoed, in connection with an idea of rewards and punishments in the afterlife, in Plato, though he also maintains that the soul, *psuchē*, is ontologically distinct from the body, *sōma*. While the body is mortal, the soul is immortal, a thesis he not only states but attempts to prove, offering several different demonstrations in the *Phaedo*, *Republic* and *Phaedrus* especially.

Then there are, in many cultures, crucial differences between deities that are uniformly or at least generally benign and those that are maleficent. In some religions the cosmos as a whole is under the rule and protection of a supreme God who stands for order and justice. In many, that God confronts the opposition of a Being who is just as important and powerful – or nearly so. Even the high God of Christianity faces the Devil, though quite how to imagine the source of evil in the world is the subject of furious theological dispute, and not just in Christianity. Where polytheisms can invoke a plurality of divine intentionalities to account for the battle between good and evil, strict monotheisms cannot use quite the same story.

If we are to scrutinise the limits of rationality, we have evidently to come to terms with this complex nexus of beliefs and practices. Many seem to imply the suspension of all the usual expectations concerning how things behave, and what causes what, that are implicit in everyday life. We can see that religion sometimes underpins ethical or moral judgements or otherwise serves to justify social and political arrangements. But even when we can appreciate that such factors may be in play, that generally provides no more than a superficial understanding of the religious phenomena in question. Much, of course, eludes any such rationalisation. Indeed whether any mode of rationalisation is possible is precisely where one of our chief challenges arises.

Attempts to explain the origin of religious belief go back to antiquity, to be sure, and this is a key point I shall endeavour to bring to bear on the whole debate. One idea concerning anthropomorphic deities was that kings or very powerful individuals had been made the objects of worship and thus turned into gods. This notion is attributed to Euhemerus at the end of the fourth century BCE, as reported in the extensive discussion of the belief in the existence of gods in Sextus Empiricus (*Against the Mathematicians* [*M.*] 9. 51).[1] Euhemerus apparently used the idea to explain the origin of Zeus himself, but there are plenty of examples of Greek legends

---

[1] Sextus lived in the second century CE and is (with Cicero) one of our most important sources for earlier Greek and Roman debates about the existence of the gods, the viability of divination and the like. We must bear in mind, however, that Sextus has his particular, sceptical, agenda, using

about mostly minor deities having originally been humans, a belief facilitated, in Greece, by the category of 'heroes' who were intermediate between
gods and humans. One such is Asclepius, whose escapades and *hubris* as a
human (when he dared to restore a dead person to life) are encapsulated
in legend, but who then became a god, worshipped in magnificent shrines
built in his honour, to which the sick came to be healed.

Parallels for such an idea of human deification exist also in ancient China
(Puett 2002 sets out much evidence on the point) and in some cases survive into modern times. Li Bing, the great third-century BCE engineer
who diverted the river Min, turning it from one dangerous river into two
highly useful ones, was and still is worshipped, sometimes covertly but
often quite openly, in a shrine that overlooks the place where he completed
this achievement. Chengis or Chinggis Khan, the mightiest of the Mon-
gol emperors, continues to be the object of worship today (Humphrey and
Onon 1996 and Humphrey and Hürelbaatar 2013), and of course many
other examples could be given.

Sextus is one of our chief sources for several other ancient Greek ideas.
The fifth-century BCE 'sophist' Prodicus is reported as claiming that what
benefits us humans is god, the sun, for example, the moon, rivers, springs
and so on.[2] Bread was named Demeter, wine Dionysus, water Poseidon, fire
Hephaestus, an idea that had some support in the common Greek practice
of using the names of certain gods to stand for what they were associated
with. Thus 'Hephaestus', for instance is used for fire (*Il.* 2 426), and when
it rains, it is Zeus that does so (Alcaeus 34, a usage even echoed in Aristotle's
Physics 198b18).

But while Prodicus' idea put the emphasis on the beneficence of the
gods, a further proposal, associated with Critias, was that the idea of the
gods stems from an invention of 'a shrewd and subtle mind' who used it to
frighten the wicked 'even if they acted, spoke or thought in secret' (Sextus
M. 9. 54).[3] The idea that the Olympian gods somehow guarantee justice
and order in the cosmos is given different expressions already in Homer
and more especially in Hesiod.[4] The new twist that Critias introduced was

---

the disagreements among earlier authorities to cast doubt on the correctness of any one purported
solution to the problems.

[2] Sextus, *M.* 9.18 and 52.

[3] Whether Critias intended to endorse these ideas is controversial, for they were put into the mouth
of Sisyphus, a character in a drama, who was, of course, in the myths associated with him, punished
for his views. However, that does not affect the main point, which is that the text is evidence that
this particular rationalisation of belief in the gods was expressed in classical Greece.

[4] The point was made much of by Lloyd-Jones (1983), who, however, rather downplays the difficulties
that this moralistic view faces in Homer at least.

to suggest that the gods were a human fiction, implying that in reality they did not exist.

Indeed the idea that there was an element of convention and cultural relativity in beliefs in the gods antedates Critias' rationalisation. In the early sixth century BCE Xenophanes said that the Ethiopians have gods that are like Ethiopians, snub-nosed and black, while the Thracians have gods like Thracians, blue-eyed and blond (Fr. 16), and he even extended that notion to other creatures in Fr. 15: 'If oxen and horses and lions had hands and could draw with their hands ... horses would represent the gods as horses and oxen as oxen'. The very idea that gods had human shape, fundamental to Greek anthropomorphic religion, was thereby undermined, as also were other aspects of the traditional conception of those divinities. Xenophanes attacks Homer and Hesiod by name in another fragment (Fr. 11) for having attributed disgraceful behaviour to the gods, 'thieving, adultery and deceiving one another', and elsewhere he mocks the Pythagorean idea of the transmigration of souls (Fr. 7). What Xenophanes himself proposed, by contrast, was an idea of god 'unlike humans in shape or in mind' (Fr. 23). God 'sees as a whole, thinks as a whole, hears as a whole' (Fr. 24). In other words, however non-anthropomorphic this God is, he nevertheless resembles humans in having cognitive capacities even though his seeing, thinking, hearing are evidently far superior to ours.

The challenge to 'traditional' notions of the gods in ancient Greece thus could have very different consequences. If Critias expresses the idea that those notions were a human invention for the purposes of social control, others, such as Xenophanes, concentrated on radical revisions of what counts as divine, debunking many elements of traditional anthropomorphism (even though god still has a body), but still keeping the notion of gods knowing and controlling things and being exemplars of moral behaviour. But a further reaction was to underline the difficulty of arriving at any reliable conception of god at all. Xenophanes himself (Fr. 34) already spoke of the difficulty of arriving at the truth of the matter, and the fifth-century 'sophist' Protagoras went further, putting it in Fr. 4 that 'concerning the gods I am unable to discover whether they exist or not, or what they are like in form: for there are many obstacles to knowledge, the obscurity of the subject and the brevity of human life'.

To express such doubts in ancient Greece was to expose yourself to a certain risk, not just of disapproval but of legal sanctions. The story reported in the late source Diogenes Laertius (9 52) that Protagoras' books were burnt is nowadays generally discounted, for there is plenty of evidence, in Plato no less, that he was held in high regard. But of course one of the charges against

Socrates was that he introduced new gods and did not recognise those that the city did. While we would say that that hardly tallies with what else we know about him (his respect for the Delphic oracle, for instance), once he was brought to trial he was set on a collision course with much popular opinion. His idealistic but arrogant stubbornness, or at the very least his lack of contrition, as his fellow citizens would have seen it, eventually led to his conviction and execution. That, at any rate, is the view promulgated by our certainly far from unbiased sources, Plato especially.

In ancient China, too, battles between traditionalists and sceptics were joined, though not ones that led to criminal prosecution. Xunzi in the third century BCE thought that those who hoped for a cure by placating the spirits were wasting their time and their resources: you will have worn out a drum and sacrificed a pig, but that will not ensure that you return to health (ch. 21). At the turn of the millennium, Wang Chong similarly attacked many common beliefs about ghosts and demons.[5] Yet such sceptical views had little impact in practice. Most Chinese remained concerned about how the dead might continue to bring ill fortune unless the proper rituals were carried out (Puett forthcoming). In that context there is a kind of hierarchy, from high gods to lesser, impermanent ones, each of whom needed to be placated in the proper fashion, and so in a manner brought under control or at least have their powers neutralised. Meanwhile, the worship of ancestors was one of the most enduring features of Chinese religion, as indeed the Jesuits discovered when, in the sixteenth century, they embarked on their mission to convert the Chinese to Christianity.

It is time now to pause and take stock of both the major similarities and differences in the experience of ancient civilisations in these matters and in the attitudes adopted to them. The idea that social and indeed cosmic order depended on divine forces can be found in both ancient China and Greece. The thought that the gods ensured that the wicked would not get away with their wickedness was common, even if it faced plenty of seemingly patent counterexamples. So to rescue the theory in the face of instances of evil people who did seem to get off scot-free, some had recourse to the supposition that their descendents would be punished in their place. Such retribution could not be disproved since it might be indefinitely postponed, although how these surrogate victims could be thought to confirm the notion that the gods are *just* was problematic. It certainly implied that responsibility for misdeeds was not individual but corporate.

[5] See, for example, *Lun Heng* 3 (*qiguai*) 73 ff., 18 (*ziran*) 365 ff., 24 (*bushi*) 482 ff., and 26 (*shizhi*) 519 ff.

But if challenges to traditional beliefs were mounted, they did not generally impinge on actual religious behaviour, the continued observance of long-established cults and rituals, in the household and the state. On that score, the main changes we can observe are to be related not so much to criticism of existing ideas as to the introduction of new ones. In the Graeco-Roman world there were first new strands of mystery religions, but then far more significantly the arrival of Christianity. In China Buddhism began to be preached already at the end of the Han, but came to be a major influence on religious belief and practice from the third century CE onwards.

We should be clear that we can do no more than speculate concerning the factors that brought about these major upheavals. Certainly the successes of both Christianity and Buddhism owe much to the way they were eventually taken up and patronised by rulers or those in the top echelons of society. But that just pushes the question back to the reasons for their taking to the new faith in the ways they did. If issues of realpolitik may have played a part, as also more general social and political factors, it is obvious that we are in no position to say what were either the necessary or the sufficient conditions for the particular changes that took place, when and where they did. It is all too easy to conclude from the eventual successes of the new religions that these were somehow inevitable. But the fluctuating fortunes of Buddhism through the centuries in China show that that is not the case, and in the Graeco-Roman world it is clear that things might have worked out very differently if Mithraism or any one of a number of other mystery religions had achieved a firmer institutional basis.[6]

The salutary lesson that this leaves us with is that (as we said before) any expectation of being able to give hard-edged explanations of spiritual phenomena is likely to be defeated. But there have, of course, been many attempts, in modern times, to come to terms with the origins, appeal and persistence of religious belief in general, which we should now endeavour to review. Among the lines of argument that have been used, some refer to

---

[6] If we ask why the momentum of physical investigations in such fields as astronomy, harmonics, zoology and anatomy appears to slow in late Graeco-Roman antiquity, the answers are again extremely complex. We must first guard against any reading back of an equivalent of the nineteenth-century dispute between 'science' and 'religion'. Many of the most prominent investigators, Galen and Ptolemy among them, held that what they were investigating, the heavenly bodies, human anatomy, nature as a whole, manifested the divine. So far from their work undermining the presence of the divine, they were convinced that it celebrated it. While they were able to arrive at what they considered satisfactory explanations of many phenomena, many of the fundamental issues, in element theory and in cosmology, remained unresolved and led, as we have seen, to a deep-seated scepticism about whether they ever would be. So there was as much of a dispute about whether research was the way ahead as there was about what it had already achieved.

evolutionary factors, others to developmental psychology or to sociology, yet others to more general constraints from the domain of cognitive science. The very variety in what has been proposed may be taken already to suggest the difficulties that any explanatory model faces.

Take, first, the invocation of evolutionary theory, driven largely by the assumption that there must surely have been some evolutionary advantage to religious beliefs of whatever kind they took. It is easy to see that the attribution of agency and intentionality to things other than the humans and animals with which we are familiar may be prudential. Better to take evasive action from an imagined predator than to wait and see whether the object feared was indeed able to attack. Yet while that may be true in the forest or the savanna, elsewhere the cost–benefit analysis of many beliefs in divine or spiritual beings works out very differently. As we have seen, Xunzi already pointed to the waste of resources involved in placating the spirits in the forlorn hope that that would bring advantage. The extravagant cost of worshipping the gods may be very damaging economically but that itself may be an important factor, in the eyes of the devout, confirming their sense of the importance and value of their beliefs.

As we discussed in chapter 2 in relation to Piaget, those who engage in studies of the psychological development of children and in what is called folk psychology more generally have been able to suggest hypotheses about the stages through which that development proceeds. In particular they have pointed to the prevalence, among children up to a certain age, of an assumption that they are surrounded by objects that are alive and possess intentions, a belief they need to modify as they achieve greater understanding and control of their environment. Given that many religions populate the world with animate beings, it might look as if the continued belief in intentional divinities is just a residual childlike delusion. Yet of course in most of their interactions in everyday life adults in every society make perfectly good use of an awareness of the, or at least a, distinction between the animate and the inanimate, as indeed they have to in order to survive. The puzzle on that account too lies in the persistence of a certain set of counterintuitive beliefs about divinities in the face not just of the evident cost in terms of resources that such beliefs entail, but also of the cognitive dissonance produced by their very counterintuitiveness.

Does sociology do any better? The idea that religion earns its keep, as it were, as a guarantor of social cohesion and order has been a favourite functionalist mode of rationalisation (e.g. Rappaport 1999). Yet that guarantee is only effective if there is a consensus on the religious or spiritual beliefs in question, and as we have seen, that faces the difficulty that criticism and scepticism are widespread and far from confined to 'advanced' literate societies.

On the face of it, appeals to cognitive science, to the idea that religious beliefs answer some profound human affective need and are subject to well-defined cognitive constraints, seem to be more promising. Atran, who has surveyed the limitations in most existing accounts of religion, himself favours the view that 'no other mode of thought and behavior deals routinely and comprehensively with the moral and existential dilemmas that panhuman emotions and cognitions force on human awareness and social life, such as death and deception' (Atran 2002: 280),[7] adding that 'as long as people share hope beyond reason, religion will persevere'.

Atran's discussion certainly serves to illuminate some of the key psychological and sociological factors in play in the creation, maintenance and spread of religious beliefs. But like all other would-be overarching accounts, it suffers from three difficulties of varying degrees of severity. The first is that it tends to exaggerate the universality of such beliefs. If religion corresponds to a 'panhuman' need, how is that some individuals can do without it? This is not just a remark that might be thought only applicable to those who have benefited from some supposed Enlightenment revolution, for as we have noted in chapter 5, already in ancient societies as well as in modern indigenous ones there are critics and sceptics, challenging the validity of religious beliefs and not so much explaining them as explaining them away.

Second, the very variety of beliefs and practices may be thought to pose a problem, for on what basis do people choose between different religions, as they evidently often do, whenever (as usually) they are aware that others do not share their own? If any religion meets the cognitive and affective needs that Atran identifies, then that by itself leaves us with no good reason for anyone to prefer one set of religious beliefs and practices over any other. That may be the case in the abstract. But of course the pressure to conform to what your own immediate group adheres to may in practice leave no room for argument.

---

[7] One may compare the functionalist view expressed long ago by Malinowski (1925: 82–3): 'Religious faith establishes, fixes, and enhances all valuable mental attitudes, such as reverence for tradition, harmony with environment, courage and confidence in the struggle with difficulties and at the prospect of death. This belief, embodied and maintained by cult and ceremonial, has an immense biological value, and so reveals to primitive man truth in the wider, pragmatic sense of the word.' However, Malinowski went on to contrast religion with 'magic', where 'gaps in [man's] knowledge and the limitations of his early power of observation and reason betray him at a crucial moment'. Yet magic too has a function, namely 'to ritualise man's optimism, to enhance his faith in the victory of hope over fear'.

Then the third point that develops from that last observation is this. If indeed we are often faced with the emotional and cognitive stresses and strains that Atran and others see as the stimulus to religiosity, then there are, of course, other resources, not religious ones, that offer a different type of response. Poetry, music and art all in their different ways provide meditations on aspects of the human predicament, and if some poetry may indeed be religious in character, that does not apply to all poetic creativity. No more do music and art necessarily appeal to or assume divine agencies. In those two cases, too, the creative processes of those who produce and enjoy them do not, of themselves, depend on subscribing to an idea of divine intentionality.

We have, then, on the one hand to acknowledge the pervasiveness of some notion of divine beings at work in the world, but on the other to see that it has been perfectly possible for individuals, and in some cases groups, to arrive at critical judgements in the matter, leading them to adhere to some notions rather than others, some practices rather than others, and at the limit deciding to adhere to none with a distinctly religious character at all.

That is not to endorse some evolutionary account of religion itself that would have it that it arose from primitive superstition and has now been, or should have been, rendered otiose by the advance of philosophy and science. The first objection that such an account encounters is that some of the most notable contributors to those advances, both philosophers and scientists, have themselves been devout believers and practitioners. That might still be explained away on the basis of the argument that those individuals were still not fully emancipated from those atavistic beliefs. But to claim that philosophy and science can in principle (if not yet in practice) provide adequate solutions to all the problems that we might face, and comfort for all the fears and anxieties that may surround us, is no more than an expression of an article of faith. We can and must agree that the actual, not just the potential, problems, the fears and anxieties, are real enough without endorsing the idea that it must be what we call religion that supplies the answers, for as I just noted, poetry, art and music offer different resources for coming to terms with those realities and for consolation. Indeed, in the case of contemporary religious fanaticism, that phenomenon is one of the major sources of our fears, no part of the answer to them. One might fondly suppose that the fanatics themselves should be able to see this if they considered humankind as a whole. But then their condemnation of large sections of humanity as infidels effectively blocks any such observation. That still leaves them with the difficulty of accounting for those massive failures of the true faith to persuade everyone of its validity, though that in turn, for them, must not be allowed to dilute the conviction in the unique truth of their own beliefs.

That said, the strength of the particular consolations on offer from religious belief and practice are generally recognised to be exceptional, and yet the price paid for this is high. As Atran (2002, 2010) and Boyer (1994, 2001, 2010) both duly note, most religions demand belief in highly counterintuitive, paradoxical, counterfactual ideas that fly in the face of our ordinary experience. God is everywhere, but also nowhere in particular, both human and yet not human (in many religions), a guarantee of the moral order which nevertheless is everywhere seen to be under threat. However, as I have argued elsewhere (2009: ch. 7) the very paradoxicality of God's ways may also be a source of strength at least in the eyes of the faithful. It is because they are such a striking exception to what we ordinarily assume that they are worth believing in. The very questionability of the account of the divine is transformed into a support for its unquestionability.[8] Thus while other poetry, music and art do not have such a high price to pay in terms of the implausibility of the conceptual framework they presuppose, they may have less of a grip on human imaginings for that very reason.

Meanwhile, another possible source of the hold that religion itself may have is usually the institutions that grow up around it. Poets, musicians and artists may sometimes form elites, but they are not organised into churches with priests standing guard over orthodoxy, sanctioning deviants, threatening unbelievers with the direst consequences of their heresies in the afterlife if not in this one. Yet that too manifests a deep ambivalence, for while those who waver may be inclined to play safe and subscribe to what the religious institutions prescribe, reflection on the merely human and social origins of those establishments may give rise to doubts and criticism. Churches, shrines, temples may, then, be a source of massive support for the beliefs and rituals practised in them, but also one of weakness if they can be seen to have had all too human origins and their holy men and women subject to all too human frailties.

Four final items on the list of the subjects I identified for this chapter, mysticism, miracles, magic and myth, all pose their distinctive problems and illustrate the tensions between what is accepted as normal and what is considered out of the ordinary. What do we mean by mysticism? One of William James's great insights was that what any given individual describes

---

[8] We may recall from chapter 2, n. 14 the points that Tertullian made when having said that 'the Son of God is dead: this is to be believed because it is absurd'. He went on: 'having been buried He rose again. This is certain because it is impossible' (*On the Flesh of Christ* ch. 5).

as a mystical experience has the character of being inaccessible to anyone else. This is not a matter of a gap between priests and laypersons, or between the initiated and the uninitiated, or between believer and sceptic, but rather of one between the person with the mystical experience and everyone else.

This is far different from the subjectivity of an ordinary sensory experience. What precisely you or I see when we look at a rainbow is private to you or to me. But in that case there is a rainbow for each of us to see. When someone reports that they have seen a vision of God, or that God has talked to them,[9] there is nothing in those experiences that anyone else can directly share. In such a case it is not that we can understand nothing of what is going on (which would mean we would be facing an exception to the principle I advanced earlier, that we can always manage <u>some</u> understanding). But when confronted with someone reporting a mystical experience, including protesting that their own descriptions do not do justice to that experience, we may well be at a loss and reduced merely to registering that they have undergone some exceptional event.

We can and do recognise that for the person who does the reporting it was a vision or an apotheosis or however it is to be classified, but we are in no position to share that experience itself. We can and do understand the words used for the experience, for they come from the ordinary natural language we use for all our experiences. But in this case they do not refer to what they normally refer to. Indeed it is usually part of the message the mystic is keen to convey, that what has happened to him or her far exceeds the limit of what is ordinarily expressible. The situation thus approximates not so much to Kuhnian incommensurable (but fully worked out) paradigms, as to the Wittgensteinian *envoi*, 'whereof one cannot speak, thereof one must be silent', or else to the solipsist's dilemma that the truth of his or her solipsism cannot be conveyed to anyone, for there is no one to whom it can be conveyed. The mystic's experience is an extreme case to remind us of the limits of intersubjectivity, but maybe just that point is all we can be said concretely to learn from the accounts of such experiences.

If the mystic is intensely private, miracles are at least sometimes events that are supposed to belong to the public domain. It is true that 'miraculous' is often used loosely as a synonym for 'wonderful' or 'awesome', for anything that excites our sense of the marvellous. But it also has a precise usage in Christian belief, where verifying that a miracle has taken place is a

---

[9] Luhrmann (2012) sets out the results of a detailed investigation of the phenomenon of subjects reporting that God talks to them from modern-day evangelical Christianity in California, research that she is now extending in a cross-cultural study to determine how the same God is experienced differently in different parts of the world.

key test for a claim to sainthood. For that verification to be complete every possible natural cause has to be ruled out. Where the natural scientist takes it as axiomatic that every event has a natural cause, the devout insist that there are exceptions, not that they are <u>uncaused</u>, but that the operational cause is divine; that is, <u>supernatural</u>. Both sceptic and believer share a sense of the need to explore every possibility of natural causation. But when faced with apparent failure, the response is quite different. The sceptic will insist that the search must continue, for a natural cause has to be there, however much it eludes human efforts to identify it. But the faithful will accept defeat with joy, as proof that it was God who was at work.

It is clear that in this context the concept of the 'supernatural' piggybacks on that of the natural, one that has its polemical history, as I have pointed out before. The Christian notion of a miracle thus turns one of the original motivations for the (pre-Christian) invention of the idea of nature on its head. While for the ancient Greek natural philosophers nature carved out a domain over which they were to be the acknowledged experts, for the devout Christian demonstrating the limitations and fallibility of that expertise was a sovereign way of proving the presence and the power of the divine. For many, 'science' today relies on an all-encompassing concept of nature out there to be investigated, though I have expressed my doubts as to whether that concept does justice to the pluralism of ideas about how the investiganda may be construed. But when that belief is combined with adherence to some religion (as with many modern scientists), 'nature' is both an article of faith, and at the same time subject to suspension, when its laws yield to the superior potency of God.

For my next topic we return to the category of the 'magical', more general than the 'miraculous' and not limited (as miracles usually were) to what was positive and beneficial. Here too the ancient origins of the term are relevant. We have references to the Magoi as either a particular tribe or a priestly group within a tribe in Persia,[10] but the term *mageia* from which we derive our 'magic' gets to be used of practices that those natural philosophers I have just mentioned criticised and rejected. In the Hippocratic text *On the Sacred Disease* the purifiers who claim to know about the 'sacred' disease, even to the point of identifying which divinity is responsible for which type, are dismissed as frauds and impostors. According to this author this disease has its nature and its cause like all other diseases, for the understanding of which there is no need for 'magic' and charlatanry. In other contexts, too,

---

[10] For Herodotus, for instance, the *magoi* are a Median tribe, who, or members of which, acted as priests and the interpreters of signs and dreams. See e.g. 1 101, 107, 120, 128, 132, 140, 7 19, 37 and 43.

such as divination, suspicion was cast on individuals by comparing them to, or calling them, 'magicians'.[11]

In fifth-century Greece the overwhelming use of the term is negative. You do not find individuals positively boasting of their magical powers. But just that development happens later in the Graeco-Roman world, when we see that the exceptional nature of magical activity could be a source of claims to special knowledge, rather than a way of undermining any such pretensions. In China, while there was no one term that is equivalent to 'magician', there were mediums (*wu*) deemed capable of controlling the weather, causing rain to fall or stopping it, and others who specialised in particular esoteric techniques (*fang shi*). These too were often marginal figures who were viewed with suspicion and sometimes with fear. Some of their claims (as we have seen) were flatly refuted, though that did not mean they were put out of business. They were evidently still needed even when their ability, their genuineness and their honesty were all called into question.

The question that was constantly raised was precisely what could or could not be achieved by whatever ordinary or extraordinary techniques were available. Even when a particular technology – in metallurgy for instance – was reasonably well understood, by trained craftsmen at least, success in getting the best results was far from guaranteed. To maximise the chance of success all sorts of procedures might be thought to be necessary or at least advisable, and these might include prayers or the utterance of spells and the ritual purification of the craftsmen themselves. We may recall the text from *Zhuangzi* 19 that I cited in chapter 3 (n. 18), where a craftsman fasts before making a bell-stand. In medicine, when a pupil was accepted by a teacher this was often marked by an initiation. In the *Lingshu* recension of the *Huangdi neijing* there is a legendary model for this, when the Thunder Duke purifies himself for three days and seals his oath by cutting his arm and smearing blood before receiving the text of the book that is put into his hands by the Yellow Emperor.[12]

Whether a particularly fortunate outcome was secured by the rites that preceded it was not something people generally felt inclined to put to the test – by seeing whether a good result could be obtained without the procedure in question. Where agriculture was concerned, such experimentation could carry considerable hazards. If, for example, it was believed that crops

---

[11] As in Oedipus' criticism of Teiresias in Sophocles' *Oedipus Tyrannus* 387 ff., where of course Oedipus himself is mistaken and Teiresias' predictions turn out to be confirmed.

[12] See *Lingshu* 48.1, 396 ff., on which see Sivin (1995c: 184–5 and n. 25). Cf. the acceptance of Chunyu Yi by his teachers described in the *Shiji* 105: 2815–16.

should be sown or planted only when the moon is waxing, you would not want to run the risk of failure by doing so when it is waning.[13] It was always safer to follow what tradition prescribed, even when doubts might be entertained and even expressed about their efficacy.

Of course, in positivist attempts to describe the grand sweep of human progress, magic and superstition played a crucial role as characteristic of primitive belief. They were contrasted with the rise of religion – the authors in question lived in societies with strong religious institutions and were often themselves believers. But the endorsement of high religion aimed to ensure that what would have been dismissed as magic in other societies was purged of any conceivable pejorative undertones, as in the case of the divine miracles we have just been discussing. Nevertheless, in the view of some positivist historians of the nineteenth century, religion was itself superseded, in certain areas if not in all, by 'science'.

The flaws in that grand picture now seem obvious to us. The idea that magic is just botched science assumes that magic aimed for efficacy, when, as I argued in chapter 2, many magical practices and beliefs have a rather different target. They are to be judged not by the criterion of effectiveness but rather by those of appropriateness or felicity. Has the ritual been performed in the proper way? The example I used before was that of the bride and groom in certain Christian weddings being showered by confetti. If one possible origin for that practice (when rice was thrown rather than confetti) may have been connected with some idea of ensuring the fertility of the married couple, that is certainly not in the minds of everyone who thought that practice was worth continuing. Rather, as I put it, the idea might be that a wedding without the confetti would not somehow be a proper wedding. Weddings being important events, with great social consequences, they should not be conducted in just any way the participants fancied, but in ways that everyone can see underlined their significance.

In such contexts the criterion is, then, felicity, and that yields a different way to understand the practices in question, one that offers an alternative to simply condemning them as the result of some naive belief that they have a direct causal effect. Yet we must acknowledge that too hard and fast a contrast between felicity and efficacy may be a mistake, for it is clearly possible for the mode of efficacy that is sought to be primarily a matter of what is felicitous. What we must certainly allow for is that what passes as

---

[13] I take this example from contemporary southern European beliefs and practices, which in many cases parallel and may even remotely echo those reported many centuries ago by Hesiod in his account of auspicious and inauspicious days.

'magic' is no simple matter, no well-defined set of phenomena serving the same purposes wherever it exists. Rather, we must be aware of the polyvalence of the term and the heterogeneity of what it may refer to. In some cases the negative or pejorative undertones allow it to be used as a term of criticism or contempt. In others the valence of the term may be neutral or even positive. In most contexts the term signals that we are dealing with experiences that lie on the borders of what is fully intelligible. Whenever that is so, it is as well to acknowledge – once again – that no matter what cognitive capacities we bring to bear, there is much that eludes us in most domains of human experience.

So I turn finally to the last topic on my agenda in this chapter, namely myth, a key concept that is involved in so many of the issues I have been discussing in these studies. Once more questions to do with cross-cultural viability have to be addressed. Once more there is a marked ambivalence in the different ways in which the concept has been deployed. On the one hand, the mythical has sometimes been equated with the unreal, the imaginary, the fictitious. On the other, since Lévi-Strauss (1970–81) especially, sets of myths have been shown to manifest a structure and what he called a logic that convey complex messages to do with fundamental problems, the human condition, the origins of the world and much else besides. On that second view there is no question of some supposed progress from 'myth' to 'reason', no question of 'myth' manifesting a failure of reason, since myths themselves have their own rationality and carry their lessons in modes of discourse that are appropriate to themselves.

The cross-cultural question has often been supposed to be a matter of definition.[14] If we take 'myths' to be traditional tales, they are to be found everywhere. But that leaves us with the question of how those traditional tales were viewed by those who told and performed them. Do the actors themselves draw a distinction – any distinction, indeed – between stories that tell of present-day events and those that deal with remote times, times quite different from those of today? Do they invoke some notion of the sacred to mark out some tales from other, profane, ones? If so, then it is a mistake to seek to homogenise discourse and have it all to be subject to an identical set of criteria for appropriateness, namely those that suit familiar, mundane transactions, though the question remains of <u>how</u> those other registers are understood and marked out by the actors themselves.

---

[14] This is a major preoccupation in Kirk's influential book (Kirk 1970), but many of the problems that the search for an agreed definition raises are aired in Buxton (1999).

In this context the anthropologist Stephen Hugh-Jones's recent discussion of the categories used by the Barasana in north-west Amazonia is exemplary and is worth quoting at length:

> The Barasana category *būkūra keti* ('old peoples' stories') is normally applied to narrated myth but can also be used to refer to other historical narratives, to genealogies and to stories about the deeds of previous generations and past clan ancestors. At the other extreme the word *basa* covers song, dance and instrumental music. The category *keti oka*, which might be translated as 'sacred, powerful speech, thought or esoteric knowledge' applies, in particular, to ritual chants ... But in a more extended sense, *keti oka* applies not only to chants and shamanic spells, but also to dance songs, to the songs latent in the melodies of Yurupari flutes, and also to ritual objects, petroglyphs and sacred sites. (Hugh-Jones 2016: 160)

This shows very elegantly, first, how the Barasana explicitly make the distinctions that they find important, second that those distinctions do not map straightforwardly onto the contrast that we draw between myth/fiction versus rational account, but third and most importantly that there can be no question of judging their categories as inadequate on the basis that they fail to correspond to those we are used to.

The history of historiography in different ancient cultures similarly reveals very different attitudes to that question and to accounts that may be given of it. For some there is a seamless continuity between ancient times and the world of the present, while others may emphasise just what a gulf separates those temporalities. Clearly neither the category of 'history' itself, nor that of writing about it (historiography), can be taken to be a cross-cultural universal.[15] As between the two ancient civilisations I take as my main objects of study, the first Chinese universal history, the *Shiji*, traces the origins of the earlier dynasties to marvellous events (virgin births, for instance) but does not explicitly mark the gap between them and later – as we should say historical – events. Those stories of origins are not labelled 'myths'. Indeed the current Chinese term for 'myth', namely *shenhua*, literally 'spirit talk', is a modern introduction.

In Greece there is, on the one hand, a perfectly neutral sense of *muthos* when it is used of stories in general. However, on the other, it could be and was used to convey that contrast I have referred to, between a 'mythical'

---

[15] Some of the variety and complexity is discussed in Teich and Müller (2005) and in Feldherr and Hardy (2011).

in the sense of fictional account, and one that lays claim to be a rational one, a *logos*, even though that term, in its turn, could be used neutrally of 'word' or story in general. The pejorative use of *muthos* and its cognates is well established in the fifth century BCE, in historiography, medicine and natural philosophy, as well as in a variety of other genres, such as drama. Yet even in Plato, who so often insists on the need for *logos* in the sense of rational account, we find that in certain contexts it and *muthos* may be interchangeable. The cosmology he presents in the *Timaeus* is described alternatively as an *eikōs logos* or as an *eikōs muthos*, where the key point is the qualification of the account as *eikōs*, 'likely' (Burnyeat 2005).

But if we endeavour to disarm the recurrent Greek polemics, we have clearly to qualify the conclusions that we might propose on where 'myth' should figure in an overall analysis of rationality. Evidently, if we are not careful, the pejorative associations of the term will act as an obstacle to any understanding of the positive messages we might otherwise pick up. The recommendation that this leads to is analogous to the tactic I have adopted on the dichotomy between the literal and the metaphorical, which was in that case to replace the category of the metaphorical with that of semantic stretch. Similarly with the modes of discourse that we as observers may wish to label 'myth' as opposed to rational account, it is imperative that we think past those labels, where the term 'narrative' will do well enough to keep our options open. That is not to say that there are no distinctions, even important ones, to be drawn in the status of different narratives dealing with different subject matter. But we must always consider first and foremost how those narratives are categorised by the actors themselves as opposed to how they may appear to us. How do the actors evaluate the claims their stories make in relation to what those stories are about and taking into account the different occasions on which they may be performed – that is, the pragmatics of the communication situation? Understanding their role is a trickier business than simply pronouncing on whether or how far they encapsulate what we may hold to be the case.

Are the key questions those of validity, even verifiability, or ones of suggestiveness? As so often in these studies I would argue that our aim should be to make the most of that suggestiveness. We should learn to attune ourselves to unfamiliar ideas and unfamiliar ways of expressing them. For that we have to unlearn some of our Western inheritance from the Greeks, though that leaves us with the questions that have been at the centre of some of my earlier discussions, namely what was truly distinctive about that legacy and more importantly what were the reasons (sociological, political, intellectual) that contributed to its taking the character it did, to its successes and its shortcomings. I shall devote my final chapter to an attempt to summarise the main results of my investigations, in particular the charting of the ambivalences of rationality.

CHAPTER 7

Conclusions
The Ambivalences of Rationality

From the outset of these investigations I have repeatedly raised questions as to the extent to which, and the ways in which, thought and reasoning vary across populations. I have resisted the suggestion that the faculties themselves differ, even while the products of their exercise undoubtedly do, not least with respect to the degree of explicitness with which their operations are made the objects of self-conscious analysis and reflection. However, much of my discussion has hinged on the issue of the applicability – that is, the validity and robustness – of certain key concepts and categories, used especially, but not exclusively, in the West. It is time now to take stock and review the outcome of those elements of our inquiry.

It is striking how often the categories in question, which are still frequently taken very much for granted, are used in polemic, to win arguments over real or imaginary opponents. In each case we tend to assume that the distinctions implied, which take diverse forms, to be sure, are all well based and essential for inquiry and understanding. Do we not need to recognise the contrasts between reality and appearance, between nature and convention or culture, between the literal and derived meanings of terms, above all between rationality and the irrational? In some cases indeed, as we have seen, such binaries have useful mundane applications in any culture or society. But in others we may slip too easily into some assumption of their universal validity and not be sufficiently on our guard against their covert use to put down the ideas of rivals, whether from our own society or from others.

Let me return to a particular example I considered in chapter 4, the way in which Plato drove a wedge between the intelligible and the perceptible and his requirement that the objects we can be said truly to understand, the Forms, must possess certain characteristics, notably that they are unchanging. To insist, as he did, that beauty itself (*auto to kalon*) is simple, pure, not subject to change, nor to coming to be, nor to perishing, is to downgrade, if not to rule out absolutely, any claims that might be made that perceptible objects can be known to be truly beautiful (*Symposium* 210e–211e, *Phaedo* 78de, 100b–e, *Republic* 479a–d). Of course he was in business fighting for values, justice especially, that he felt to be threatened in the society in which he lived, the one that condemned Socrates to death, and his dialogues are testimony to his modifying his position on certain aspects of his metaphysics, including on the status of particulars. Nevertheless both the excesses of his claims and the hold they had on subsequent Western thought obviously cast a long shadow over those aspects of the legacy of ancient Greece. The ancient Chinese, we noted, for whom change is omnipresent, were not tempted to postulate an unchanging intelligible world, though to be sure we do not need to reflect on their ideas to become aware of some of the perils of Platonism.

Of course we do not, indeed cannot, abstain from judgement altogether. Those who have insisted that no description can be entirely theory-free, nor indeed entirely value-free, have a point with which I agree. But there is, then, all the more reason to be not just critical, but self-critical, especially where our own fundamental category distinctions are concerned. We have seen, or at least I have argued, that it is possible to do cosmology and to explore the physical world without invoking a concept of nature, indeed that it may be preferable to do so insofar as the notion that there are stable distinct natures out there for us to reveal may prejudge the issue of the character of our explananda – of what it is precisely we are trying to explain. The same point applies to the basic assumption, not confined to Plato, that what we are targeting is an underlying reality to be sharply contrasted with the appearances, for there are subjects where no such assumption is well grounded, where we have to be content with accepting that the appearances are the only reality in sight.

When it comes to the pair rational/irrational, my analysis has been severely deflationary. It is not that there are never any grounds to invoke that contrast. As we have noted, there is an obvious utility in checking chains of argument for consistency. But if it is one thing to diagnose inconsistency as irrational, it is quite another to assess the reasonableness or otherwise of the basic premises or assumptions of an inquiry, a theory, even a whole ontology or cosmology. Often and especially in the West the dichotomy has been deployed polemically, serving as a prime weapon to defeat opponents, whose ideas and practices, once labelled 'irrational', can be disqualified from serious consideration. It is certainly true that we have sometimes to admit bafflement at beliefs and behaviour that contravene our ordinary assumptions. But our bafflement should not be taken to imply the folly of the individuals or groups concerned, let alone that they are beyond all comprehension.

We can and should watch out for their and our mistakes, both in the premises entertained and in inferences from them, both in relation to what are represented as facts and in the theories built on them – a point that applies to our reasonings just as much as to anyone else's. But that vigilance involves hard work, harder work than a quick verdict of irrationality generally permits, and that is particularly likely to be the case when there is some implicit assumption that our own views, by contrast to those we criticise, manifest no shred of the irrational. If we pride ourselves on our capacity for self-criticism, we must practise that, identifying indeed the obstacles it always faces and recognising that we are certainly not alone in the ability to cultivate such reflexiveness.

Where argument is concerned, I have drawn attention to the difference it may make when second-order concepts of linguistic categories are available, and to further differences in the degree of explicitness with which argumentative techniques are identified. Once such concepts can be appealed to directly, that may prove a powerful weapon of persuasion and a way of claiming victory in debate (polemic again). It is, however, important to register first that such explicitness is not confined to literate societies – as we illustrated by referring, for example, to Gluckman's discussion of the Barotse. Second, certain characteristic flaws in reasoning (the confirmation bias, for instance) are widespread across societies of every type, including those where formal logic has been the subject of detailed academic study. Then third, and more generally, even all the tools that formal logic can equip us with are no guarantee that reasoning will be sound. If I am right about the pervasiveness of semantic stretch, then the hoped-for univocity that is a necessary condition for valid inference may be attainable far more rarely and in more limited contexts than is generally assumed.

In the West we owe the inauguration of such a study in the first instance to the ancient Greeks, where Aristotle was the first to attempt a systematic formal analysis of argumentation. But we have found that often the new understandings these Greeks achieved, and the new concepts they forged, were a two-edged sword. Their strength is that they allowed greater self-consciousness in the conduct of inquiry and persuasion. But their weakness was the temptation to dictate how, ideally at least, investigation should be pursued, to foreclose other perceptions both of how to go about inquiry and of what was there to be inquired into – a temptation that persists in certain ambitions even today.

Much as we owe to the advance of science, any incipient triumphalism about that has to be tempered by a recognition first of the limits of its reach, and second of the increased dangers that have come in its wake. There is so much in physics and cosmology, in biology and psychology, that we do not currently understand and even may never do so. True, we have effective methods that have achieved notable results and we are constantly striving to devise new ones. Some of those methods stem from the endeavours of the ancient Greeks; others owe much to India, to Islam and especially to China, which was, after all, responsible for three of the greatest discoveries that have influenced the development of modern science and technology: the compass, gunpowder and the printing press. Although much talk of 'the' Scientific and 'the' Industrial Revolutions involves drastic oversimplifications, the complex changes that underpin modernity are undeniable. Certainly material progress should be celebrated even while the grotesquely unequal distribution of its benefits is to be deplored. The technology that enables us to explore space is also the technology of weapons of mass destruction.

Both ethnography and history have expanded our appreciation of the vast variety of human perceptions of the world and of ways of living in it; of different views of the human predicament and of responses to it; of different modes of physicality and interiority, as Descola put it; of multinaturalism and perspectivism, as in Viveiros de Castro; and of other contrasting ontologies such as were articulated in ancient Greece and China, not to speak of later societies. Yet the lessons that can be drawn from all this diversity have scarcely begun to be fully appreciated, for that in my view depends on a due recognition both of the commonalities in human cognitive capacities, and of the differences in their deployment. In some contexts the dangers of Western intellectual imperialism seem especially prominent, when that implies that we have some monopoly of the wherewithal to arrive at a correct understanding – of ourselves, of other humans and of the world around us.

My argument has been that a more fruitful reaction to what has sometimes been dismissed with the label of the irrational is to investigate what may be said in favour of beliefs and practices that at first sight seem so counterintuitive to us. Encountering puzzling ontologies, our reaction should not be swift dismissal but a realisation of a possible opportunity for exploration. We should attempt to look at the issues from others' points of view, entertain multiple perspectives on the phenomena, including on the values attached to them, and accept the multidimensionality of reality itself. Yet of course we may not ultimately succeed in our endeavours, and that is certainly the case when it is assumed, incorrectly, that the test for that is identifying with those others.

Where our interlocutors speak and act in ways that imply that agency and intentionality are not limited to the animate beings we are familiar with, but include, for example, the gods, spirits, ghosts and demons we discussed in chapter 6, we should ask what work those beliefs and actions do in the business of making sense of life, how they are brought to bear to resolve the predicaments of the human condition and what they can tell us about how that human condition itself has been understood. Efficacy, we said, is not always the target, for sometimes appropriateness and felicity are. The aim should, then, be to exploit these alternatives as resources for our explorations of different humans' ways of being in the world, for to be sure we have no unique access to a definitively supreme set of answers to that question. There is, after all, no one exclusive solution to the problem of how, as humans, we may flourish.

Of course a sceptical and critical stance is not just desirable, but necessary. We said we should be wary of jumping to conclusions about others' mistakes. But we also need constantly to be on the alert to the possibilities of deception, of manipulation – of people or of what passes as the facts of the case – of false consciousness and ideological blindness, in our dealings with our interlocutors and in their dealings with their fellows, whether from their own particular group or from outside it.

For any species to survive it will need efficient mechanisms to detect predators and prey. In the kind of global society we live in today we face rather different, more insidious and more overwhelming kinds of threats. Let me conclude with some brief remarks about two especially, namely fanaticism and blind self-interest. First, there are those who would wipe us out for not adhering to their religious beliefs, a trait that is not confined to contemporary fanatics but one that echoes the pogroms that have punctuated the whole of human history in the name of different gods and different faiths. At the end of his *Nicomachean Ethics* Aristotle already put it that arguments are not enough to make people good.[1] It is not shame that makes people behave, but rather the fear of punishment.[2] But then, who

---

[1] 'Now if arguments were enough to make people good, then, as Theognis said, they would justly have won many and great rewards . . . But as things are, while they seem to have power to encourage and spur on liberal-minded young men . . . they are powerless to encourage the mass to noble behaviour. For they [the many] do not naturally obey the sense of shame, but only fear, and they refrain from evil deeds, not because the deeds are shameful, but because of the penalties involved' (*Nicomachean Ethics* 1179b4–13).

[2] The proper role of punishments in social control is also a recurrent theme in early Chinese thought, with those such as Hanfeizi associated with the *Fa Jia* (Lineage of Law or Legalists) especially insisting

is to decide on the punishments that are just, when the fanatics themselves see their role as punishing the unbelievers?

We noted at the outset that a necessary condition for mutual intelligibility is at least a desire to understand. That is not in the minds of the fanatics who proceed on the assumption that it is easy to identify those who do not adhere to the one true faith – who thereby forfeit any right to be heard, even any right to exist. Even while we agree with Aristotle on the weakness of reason, we have, for sure, to use it as best we can to put the case for the values we hold dear, even while we recognise that we are not infallible and indeed that all our preconceptions are revisable. Abstaining from dogmatism may make us seem weak, but it should rather be a source of strength, as a sure sign of what separates us from the fanatics. Others' deafness to reason is no grounds for our abandoning it. Rather, we should do our utmost to create the conditions where the goal of understanding others is recognised as an important value, and for sure those conditions will include the practice of open-ended unprejudiced discussion and debate.

Second, and far more pervasively, there is blind selfishness, by which I mean especially those in government or just simply in national or multinational corporations who are blinkered by self-interest from perceiving and doing what needs to be done to prevent the human race as a whole from destroying the environment on which we all depend. Those of us who lived through the Second World War assumed naively that a future not plagued by racism, intolerance, injustice and inequality was within our grasp. Such hopes have been utterly dashed. Developing countries and developed ones alike appear unable or unwilling to see what the consequences of a failure to act together to reverse catastrophic climate change will be. And when we do see them, there appear to be insurmountable obstacles to achieving united action. Or so they are represented by those who assume that doing nothing is an option. Meanwhile, where rapidly growing inequalities are concerned, there is not even a consensus on their unfairness nor on the vital necessity that such trends have to be reversed, not just a moral point, but one that is arguably in the self-interest of the privileged themselves. Yet it is commonly supposed that the success of the successful stems in part from their ruthless egotism.

In both cases the major problems relate, to be sure, to national and international politics, to the institutions on which we rely, to the conflicting

---

on the need for the severest sanctions. Confucius, however, thought it better that the laws should not be written down and made public, on the grounds that that would discourage people from internalising their sense of right and wrong (*Zuozhuan* Zhao 29: a similar view is also expressed in the *Daodejing* associated with the legendary Laozi).

values that we bring to bear and to the righteousness with which many claim their values to be the only ones to be justified, even, some would say, god-given. Such issues far transcend the abstract intellectual discussion I have undertaken in these studies. But if the problems of finding solutions to geopolitical crises are evident – the weaknesses of international institutions, the disinclination of the major powers or of bodies within them to moderate their self-interest for the sake of the common good – then we may nevertheless remark that a necessary condition for any progress in the matter is a better understanding of where human reasoning may go astray, and that can be studied among individuals and groups throughout history and across the globe. We need to strike a balance, between a respect for others' views and a sense that all must be subject to scrutiny, combined with an absolute determination in our insistence that there must be limits to a tolerance of the intolerant. As humans we are all of us equipped with truly remarkable cognitive capacities, though we do not always use our conceptual tools wisely. The fact that they have served our predecessors well may lead us to drop our guard and fail to reflect critically on their shortcomings. In that regard it is my hope that these critical examinations of some of our typical deep-seated assumptions, categories and methods may make a modest contribution to our self-awareness.

Glossary of Chinese Terms

bian¹ 辯   dispute
bian² 辨   distinguish
bushi 卜筮   divination by turtle and milfoil
dao 道   the Way
di 地   earth
fa jia 法家   the School of Law
fang shi 方士   esoteric practitioners
fei 非   is not, wrong
gaitian 蓋天   'canopy heaven'
huntian 渾天   'enveloping heaven'
jia 家   lineage, family
jiashi 假使   falsely supposing
junzi 君子   'gentleman'
li 理   pattern
lun 論   discourse
ming jia 名家   'School of Names'
qi 氣   breath, energy
qiguai 奇怪   'strange and wonderful things'
qing 清   clear
qiwulun 齊物論   the sorting that evens things out
ren 人   human
shenhua 神話   'myth'
shi 是   is, right
shizhi 實知   'true knowledge'
shou 壽   long life
shu shu 數術   calculations and methods
shui 水   water
shuo nan 說難   the difficulties of persuasion
suanshu 算術   art of reckoning
tian 天   heaven

tiandi 天地	heaven and earth
tianxia 天下	below heaven
tu 土	earth
wanwu 萬物	the myriad things
wu 巫	mediums
wu xing 五行	five phases
xiaoren 小人	petty person
xing 性	characteristics
yang 陽	positive principle: bright
yi si 疑似	spurious resemblances
yin 陰	negative principle: dark
you 有	'there is', 'have'
youshui 遊說	wandering persuaders
yu yan 寓言	'lodge sayings'
yue 曰	means, says
ziran 自然	spontaneous, 'self-so'

Notes on Editions

For Greek and Latin texts I use the editions specified in the fourth edition of the *Oxford Classical Dictionary*, ed. S. Hornblower, A. Spawforth and E. Eidinow (Oxford 2012).

Chinese texts are generally cited according to the standard editions. For example, I use the Harvard-Yenching Institute series editions of the *Mengzi*, *Mozi*, *Xunzi* (where I adopt the chapter subdivisions in Knoblock 1988–94) and *Zhuangzi*. I use the University of Hong Kong Institute of Chinese Studies editions of *Daodejing*, *Hanfeizi*, *Lunyu* and *Yijing*, and the *Zhonghua shuju* edition of the *Shiji*. For the *Zhoubi suanjing* I use the edition of Qian Baocong, *Suanjing shishu* (Beijing 1963).

I cite other texts from the following editions:

Huainanzi in the edition of Chen Qiyou (Shanghai 1958).
Huangdi neijing (*ling shu* and *su wen*) in the edition of Ren Yingqiu (Beijing 1986).
Lun Heng in that of Liu Pansui (Beijing 1957).
Lüshi chunqiu in that of Chen Qiyou (Shanghai 1984), using the section subdivisions in Knoblock and Riegel 2000.
Zuozhuan in the edition of Yang Bojun, 4 vols. (Beijing 1981), cited by Duke and Year.

All modern works are cited by author's name and date of publication. Full details are to be found in the Bibliography that follows.

Bibliography

This gives details of all the books and articles to which I refer, together with a brief selection of other texts that discuss related problems and have influenced my thinking.

Anton, J. P. (ed.) (1980) *Science and the Sciences in Plato* (New York).

Atran, S. (1990) *Cognitive Foundations of Natural History* (Cambridge).

Atran, S. (1998) 'Folk biology and the anthropology of science: cognitive universals and cultural particulars', *Behavioral and Brain Sciences* 21: 547–69.

Atran, S. (2002) *In Gods We Trust: The Evolutionary Landscape of Religion* (Oxford).

Atran, S. (2010) *Talking to the Enemy: Faith, Brotherhood and the (Un)making of Terrorists* (New York).

Atran, S., Medin, D. L. and Ross, N. (2004) 'Evolution and devolution of knowledge: a tale of two biologies', *Journal of the Royal Anthropological Institute* 10: 395–420.

Avital, E. and Jablonka, E. (2000) *Animal Traditions: Behavioural Inheritance in Evolution* (Cambridge).

Barker, A. (1989) *Greek Musical Writings II: Harmonic and Acoustic Theory* (Cambridge).

Barker, A. (2000) *Scientific Method in Ptolemy's Harmonics* (Cambridge).

Barkow, J. H., Cosmides, L. and Tooby, J. (eds.) (1992) *The Adapted Mind: Evolutionary Psychology and the Generation of Culture* (Oxford).

Barnes, S. Barry (1973) 'The comparison of belief-systems: anomaly versus falsehood', in Horton and Finnegan (1973), pp. 182–98.

Barnes, S. Barry (1974) *Scientific Knowledge and Sociological Theory* (London).

Barnes, S. Barry and Bloor, D. (1982) 'Relativism, rationalism and the sociology of knowledge', in Hollis and Lukes (1982), pp. 21–47.

Baron-Cohen, S. (2003) *The Essential Difference: Men, Women and the Extreme Male Brain* (London).

Bartha, P. F. A. (2010) *By Parallel Reasoning: The Construction and Evaluation of Analogical Arguments* (Oxford).

Bateson, P. and Gluckman, P. (2011) *Plasticity, Robustness, Development and Evolution* (Cambridge).

Bellah, R. N. (2005) 'What is axial about the axial age?' *Archives européennes de sociologie* 46: 69–89.

Bellah, R. N. (2011) *Religion in Human Evolution* (Cambridge, MA).

Berryman, S. (2009) *The Mechanical Hypothesis in Ancient Greek Natural Philosophy* (Cambridge).

Billig, M. (1996) *Arguing and Thinking*, 2nd edn (1st edn 1987) (Cambridge).

Blackburn, S. (2008) *The Oxford Dictionary of Philosophy*, revised edn (Oxford).

Bloom, A. (1981) *The Linguistic Shaping of Thought. A Study in the Impact of Language in Thinking in China and the West* (Hillsdale, NJ).

Boas, F. (1930) *The Religion of the Kwakiutl Indians*, Part 2, Columbia University Contributions to Anthropology 10 (New York).

Boesch, C. (1996) 'The emergence of cultures in wild chimpanzees', in Runciman, Maynard Smith and Dunbar (1996), 251–68.

Boesch, C. and Boesch, H. (1984) 'Possible causes of sex differences in the use of natural hammers by wild chimpanzees', *Journal of Human Evolution* 13: 415–40.

Bohannan, P. (1957) *Justice and Judgment among the Tiv* (Oxford).

Bourdieu, P. (2004) *Science of Science and Reflexivity* (trans. by R. Nice of *Science de la science et réflexivité*, Paris, 2001) (Cambridge).

Bowen, A. C. (2001) 'La scienza del cielo nel periodo pretolemaico', in S. Petruccioli (ed.), *Storia della scienza*, vol. 1, Enciclopedia Italiana (Rome) sez. 4, ch. 21, 806–39.

Bowen, A. C. (2002) 'Simplicius and the early history of Greek planetary theory', *Perspectives on Science* 10: 155–67.

Boyd, R. and Richerson, P. J. (2005) *The Origin and Evolution of Cultures* (Oxford).

Boyd, R., Richerson, P. J. and Henrich, J. (2011) 'The cultural niche: why social learning is essential for human cognition', *Proceedings of the National Academy of Sciences* 108 (Suppl. 2) 10918–25.

Boyer, P. (ed.) (1993) *Cognitive Aspects of Religious Symbolism* (Cambridge).

Boyer, P. (1994) *The Naturalness of Religious Ideas: A Cognitive Theory of Religion* (Berkeley).

Boyer, P. (2001) *Religion Explained* (New York).

Boyer, P. (2010) 'Why evolved cognition matters to understanding cultural cognitive variations', *Interdisciplinary Science Reviews* 35: 376–86.

Bray, F., Dorofeeva-Lichtmann, V. and Métailié, G. (eds.) (2007) *Graphics and Text in the Production of Technical Knowledge in China: The Warp and the Weft* (Leiden).

Bronkhorst, J. (1999) *Why Is There Philosophy in India?*, Royal Netherlands Academy of Arts and Sciences (Amsterdam).

Bronkhorst, J. (2002) 'Discipliné par le débat', in L. Bansat-Boudon and J. Scheid (eds.), *Le disciple et ses maîtres* (Paris), pp. 207–25.

Bronkhorst, J. (2007) 'Modes of debate and refutation of adversaries in classical and medieval India: a preliminary investigation', *Antiquorum Philosophia* 1: 269–80.

Burkert, W. (1985) *Greek Religion* (trans. by J. Raffan of *Griechische Religion der archaischen und klassischen Epoche*, Stuttgart, 1977) (Oxford).

Burnyeat, M. (1994) 'Enthymeme: Aristotle on the logic of persuasion', in D. J. Furley and A. Nehamas (eds.), *Aristotle's Rhetoric: Philosophical Essays* (Princeton), pp. 3–55.

Burnyeat, M. (2000) 'Plato on why mathematics is good for the soul', in T. Smiley (ed.), *Mathematics and Necessity*, Proceedings of the British Academy 103 (Oxford), pp. 1–81.

Burnyeat, M. (2005) 'Eikōs Muthos', *Rhizai* 2: 143–65.

Butterfield, H. (1949) *The Origins of Modern Science 1300–1800* (London).

Buxton, R. G. A. (ed.) (1999) *From Myth to Reason? Studies in the Development of Greek Thought* (Oxford).

Byrne, R. W. and Whiten, A. (eds.) (1988) *Machiavellian Intelligence* (Oxford).

Carneiro da Cunha, M. (2009) *'Culture' and Culture: Traditional Knowledge and Intellectual Rights* (Chicago).

Carruthers, P. (1996) *Language, Thought and Consciousness* (Cambridge).

Catchpole, C. K. and Slater, P. J. B. (2008) *Bird Song*, 2nd edn (1st edn 1995) (Cambridge).

Chang, H. (2012) *Is Water H$_2$O? Evidence, Realism and Pluralism* (Dordrecht).

Changeux, J.-P. (1985) *Neuronal Man* (trans. by L. Garey of *L'homme neuronal*, Paris, 1983) (New York).

Charbonnier, P., Salmon, G. and Skafish, P. (eds.) (2017) *Comparative Metaphysics: Ontology after Anthropology* (London).

Chemla, K. (2012a) 'Historiography and history of mathematical proof: a research programme', in Chemla (2012b), pp. 1–68.

Chemla, K. (ed.) (2012b) *The History of Mathematical Proof in Ancient Traditions* (Cambridge).

Chemla, K. (2012c) 'Reading proofs in Chinese commentaries: algebraic proofs in an algorithmic context', in Chemla (2012b), pp. 423–86.

Chemla, K. and Guo Shuchun (2004) *Les neuf chapitres. Le classique mathématique de la Chine ancienne et ses commentaires* (Paris).

Cheney, D. L. and Seyfarth, R. M. (1990) *How Monkeys See the World* (Chicago).

Chomsky, N. (2006) *Language and Mind*, 3rd edn (1st edn 1968) (Cambridge).

Cohen, H. Floris (1994) *The Scientific Revolution: A Historiographical Inquiry* (Chicago).

Cohen, H. Floris (2015) *The Rise of Modern Science Explained: A Comparative History* (Cambridge).

Cole, M., Gay, J., Glick, J. A. and Sharp, D. W. (1971) *The Cultural Context of Learning and Thinking* (New York).

Cooper, W. S. (2001) *The Evolution of Reason: Logic as a Branch of Biology* (Cambridge).

Cosmides, L. and Tooby, J. (1992) 'Cognitive adaptations for social exchange', in Barkow, Cosmides and Tooby (1992), pp. 163–228.

Cosmides, L. and Tooby, J. (1994) 'Origins of domain specificity: the evolution of functional organization', in Hirschfeld and Gelman (1994), pp. 85–116.

Crain, S. (2012) *The Emergence of Meaning* (Cambrige).

Crombie, A. C. (1994) *Styles of Scientific Thinking in the European Tradition*, 3 vols. (London).

Cullen, C. (1993) 'A Chinese Eratosthenes of the flat earth' (appendix), in Major (1993), pp. 269–90.

Cullen, C. (1996) *Astronomy and Mathematics in China: The Zhou Bi Suan Jing* (Cambridge).

Cullen, C. (2007) 'Actors, networks and "disturbing spectacles" in institutional science: 2nd century Chinese debates on astronomy', *Antiquorum Philosophia* 1: 237–67.

Cuomo, S. (2001) *Ancient Mathematics* (London).

Dascal, M. (1998) 'The study of controversies and the theory and history of science', *Science in Context* 11: 147–54.

Dascal, M. and Chang, H.-L. (eds.) (2007) *Traditions of Controversy* (Amsterdam).

Daston, L. and Galison, P. (2007) *Objectivity* (New York).

Daston, L. and Lunbeck, E. (eds.) (2011) *Histories of Scientific Observation* (Chicago).

Daston, L. and Mitman, G. (eds.) (2005) *Thinking with Animals: New Perspectives on Anthropomorphism* (New York).

Davidson, D. (2001) *Essays on Actions and Events*, 2nd edn (1st edn 1980) (Oxford).

Davidson, D. (2004) *Problems of Rationality* (Oxford).

De Jong, W. R. and Betti, A. (2010) 'The classical model of science: a millennia-old model of scientific rationality', *Synthèse* 174, 2: 185–203.

Derrida, J. (1982) *Margins of Philosophy* (trans. by A. Bass of *Marges de la philosophie*, Paris, 1972) (Chicago).

Descola, P. (1996) *The Spears of Twilight* (trans. by J. Lloyd of *Les lances du crépuscule*, Paris, 1993) (London).

Descola, P. (2013) *Beyond Nature and Culture* (trans. by J. Lloyd of *Par delà nature et culture*, Paris, 2005) (Chicago).

Detienne, M. and Vernant, J.-P. (1978) *Cunning Intelligence in Greek Culture and Society* (trans. by J. Lloyd of *Les ruses de l'intelligence: La mètis des grecs*, Paris, 1974) (Hassocks).

Diller, H. (1932) 'Opsis adēlōn ta phainomena', *Hermes* 67: 14–42.

Dodds, E. R. (1951) *The Greeks and the Irrational* (Berkeley).

Donald, M. (1991) *Origins of the Modern Mind* (Cambridge, MA).

Donald, M. (2001) *A Mind So Rare: The Evolution of Human Consciousness* (New York).

Dor, D. and Jablonka, E. (2001) 'How language changed the genes: toward an explicit account of the evolution of language', in J. Trabant and S. Ward (eds.), *New Essays on the Origin of Language* (Berlin), pp. 149–75.

Duhem, P. (1908) 'ΣΩZEIN TA ΦAINOMENA', *Annales de philosophie chrétienne* 6: 113–39, 277–302, 352–77, 482–514, 561–92.

Dunbar, R. I. M. (1998) 'The social brain hypothesis', *Evolutionary Anthropology* 6: 178–90.

Dunbar, R. I. M. (1999) 'Culture, honesty and the freerider problem', in R. Dunbar, C. Knight and C. Power (eds.), *The Evolution of Culture* (Edinburgh), pp. 194–213.

Dunbar, R. I. M. (2009) 'The social brain hypothesis and its implications for social evolution', *Annals of Human Biology* 36, 5: 562–72.

Dunn, J. (1968) 'The identity of the history of ideas', *Philosophy* 43: 85–104.

Dupré, J. (2002) *Humans and Other Animals* (Oxford).

Eisenstadt, S. N. (1982) 'The axial age: the emergence of transcendental visions and the rise of clerics', *Archives européennes de sociologie* 23: 294–314.

Eisenstadt, S. N. (ed.) (1986) *The Origins and Diversity of Axial Age Civilizations* (Albany, NY).

Evans, J. St. B. T. (1989) *Bias in Human Reasoning: Causes and Consequences* (Hove).

Evans, N. and Levinson, S. C. (2009) 'The myth of language universals: language diversity and its importance for cognitive science', *Behavioral and Brain Sciences* 32: 429–92.

Evans-Pritchard, E. E. (1937) *Witchcraft, Oracles and Magic among the Azande* (Oxford).

Evans-Pritchard, E. E. (1956) *Nuer Religion* (Oxford).

Everett, D. L. (2005) 'Cultural constraints on grammar and cognition in Pirahã', *Current Anthropology* 46: 621–34 and 641–6.

Fauconnier, G. and Turner, M. (2002) *The Way We Think* (New York).

Feldherr, A. and Hardy, G. (eds.) (2011) *The Oxford History of Historical Writing*, vol. 1 (Oxford).

Finley, M. I. (1983) *Politics in the Ancient World* (Cambridge).

Fowler, R. L. (2011) '*Mythos* and *Logos*', *Journal of Hellenic Studies* 131: 45–66.

Frede, M. and Striker, G. (eds.) (1996) *Rationality in Greek Thought* (Oxford).

Furley, D. J. (1987) *The Greek Cosmologists*, vol. 1 (Cambridge).

Gellner, E. (1973) 'The savage and the modern mind', in Horton and Finnegan (1973), pp. 162–81.

Gellner, E. (1974) *Legitimation of Belief* (Cambridge).

Gellner, E. (1985) *Relativism and the Social Sciences* (Cambridge).

Gellner, E. (1988) *Plough, Sword and Book* (London).

Gellner, E. (1992) *Reason and Culture: The Historic Role of Rationality and Rationalism* (Oxford).

Gernet, J. (1985) *China and the Christian Impact* (trans. by J. Lloyd of *Chine et christianisme*, Paris, 1982) (Cambridge).

Gigerenzer, G. and Goldstein, D. G. (1996) 'Reasoning the fast and frugal way: models of bounded rationality', *Psychological Review* 103: 650–69.

Gigerenzer, G. and Todd, P. M. (1999) *Simple Heuristics That Make Us Smart* (Oxford).

Gluckman, M. (1965) *Politics, Law and Ritual in Tribal Society* (Oxford).

Gluckman, M. (1967) *The Judicial Process among the Barotse of Northern Rhodesia* 2nd edn (1st edn 1955) (Manchester).

Gluckman, M. (1972) *The Ideas in Barotse Jurisprudence* 2nd edn (1st edn 1965) (Manchester).

Goldin, P. R. (2008) 'The myth that China has no creation myth', *Monumenta Serica* 56: 1–22.

Goodman, N. (1978) *Ways of Worldmaking* (Hassocks).

Goody, J. (1977) *The Domestication of the Savage Mind* (Cambridge).

Goody, J. (1986) *The Logic of Writing and the Organization of Society* (Cambridge).

Goody, J. (1987) *The Interface between the Written and the Oral* (Cambridge).

Graham, A. C. (1978) *Later Mohist Logic, Ethics and Science* (London).

Graham, A. C. (1981) *Chuang-tzu: The Seven Inner Chapters* (London).

Graham, A. C. (1986) *Yin Yang and the Nature of Correlative Thinking* (Singapore).

Graham, A. C. (1989) *Disputers of the Tao* (La Salle, IL).

Griffin, D. R. (1984) *Animal Thinking* (Cambridge, MA).

Griffin, D. R. (1992) *Animal Minds* (Chicago).

Gumperz, J. J. and Levinson, S. C. (eds.) (1996) *Rethinking Linguistic Relativity* (Cambridge).

Hacking, I. (1975) *The Emergence of Probability* (Cambridge).

Hacking, I. (1992) '"Style" for historians and philosophers', *Studies in History and Philosophy of Science* 23, 1: 1–20.

Hacking, I. (2007) 'Natural kinds: rosy dawn, scholastic twilight', in A. O'Hear (ed.), *Philosophy of Science* (Cambridge), pp. 203–39.

Hacking, I. (2009) *Scientific Reason* (Taipei).

Hacking, I. (2012) '"Language, truth and reason" 30 years later', *Studies in History and Philosophy of Science* 43, 4: 599–609.

Hadot, P. (2006) *The Veil of Isis: An Essay on the History of the Idea of Nature* (trans. by M. Chase of *Le voile d'Isis: Essai sur l'histoire de l'idée de nature*, Paris, 2004) (Cambridge, MA).

Hansen, M. H. (1983) *The Athenian Ecclesia* (Copenhagen).

Hansen, M. H. (1991) *The Athenian Democracy in the Age of Demosthenes* (Oxford).

Harbsmeier, C. (1998 *Science and Civilisation in China*, vol. 7 part 1, *Language and Logic* (Cambridge).

Harman, G. (1986) *Change in View: Principles of Reasoning* (Cambridge, MA).

Harper, D. (1998) *Early Chinese Medical Literature: The Mawangdui Manuscripts* (London).

Havelock, E. (1963) *Preface to Plato* (Oxford).

Havelock, E. (1976) *Origins of Western Literacy* (Toronto).

Havelock, E. (1982) *The Literate Revolution in Greece and Its Cultural Consequences* (Princeton).

Havelock, E. (1986) *The Muse Learns to Write: Reflections on Orality and Literacy from Antiquity to the Present* (New Haven).

Heath, T. L. (1921) *A History of Greek Mathematics*, 2 vols. (Oxford).

Henrich, J., Heine, S. J. and Norenzayan, A. (2010) 'The weirdest people in the world?', *Behavioral and Brain Sciences* 33: 61–83.

Hirschfeld, L. A. and Gelman, S. A. (eds.) (1994) *Mapping the Mind: Domain Specificity in Cognition and Culture* (Cambridge).

Hollis, M. (1987) *The Cunning of Reason* (Cambridge).

Hollis, M. and Lukes, S. (eds.) (1982) *Rationality and Relativism* (Oxford).

Holyoak, K. J. and Morrison, R. G. (eds.) (2005) *The Cambridge Handbook of Thinking and Reasoning* (Cambridge).

Holyoak, K. J. and Thagard, P. (1995) *Mental Leaps: Analogy in Creative Thought* (Cambridge, MA).

Hopkins, K. (1980) 'Brother–sister marriage in Roman Egypt', *Comparative Studies in Society and History* 22: 303–54.

Horton, R. and Finnegan, R. (eds.) (1973) *Modes of Thought* (London).

Hsu, E. (2010) *Pulse Diagnosis in Early Chinese Medicine: The Telling Touch* (Cambridge).

Hudson, L. (1966) *Contrary Imaginations* (London).

Huff, T. E. (2011) *Intellectual Curiosity and the Scientific Revolution: A Global Perspective* (Cambridge).

Hugh-Jones, S. (2016) 'Writing on stone; writing on paper: myth, history and memory in NW Amazonia', *History and Anthropology* 27: 154–82.

Humboldt, W. von (1988) *On Language: The Diversity of Human Language-Structure and Its Influence on the Mental Development of Mankind* (trans. by P. Heath of *Über die Verschiedenheit des menschlichen Sprachbaues und ihren Einfluss auf die geistige Entwickelung des Menschengeschlechts*, Berlin, 1836) (Cambridge).

Humle, T. and Matsuzawa, T. (2002) 'Ant-dipping among the chimpanzees of Bossou, Guinea, and some comparisons with other sites', *American Journal of Primatology* 58: 133–48.

Humphrey, C. and Hürelbaatar, Ujeed (2013) *A Monastery in Time: The Making of Mongolian Buddhism* (Chicago).

Humphrey, C. and Onon, Urgunge (1996) *Shamans and Elders: Experience, Knowledge, and Power among the Daur Mongols* (Oxford).

Humphrey, N. (1976) 'The social function of intellect', in P. P. G. Bateson and R. A. Hinde (eds.), *Growing Points in Ethology* (Cambridge), pp. 303–17.

Humphrey, N. (1992) *A History of the Mind* (London).

Humphrey, N. (2011) *Soul Dust* (Princeton).

Humphreys, S. C. (1985) 'Social relations on stage: witnesses in classical Athens', in S. C. Humphreys, *The Discourse of Law* (London), pp. 313–69.

Ierodiakonou, K. (2005) 'Ancient thought experiments: a first approach', *Ancient Philosophy* 25: 125–40.

Ingold, T. (2000) *The Perception of the Environment* (London).

Jablonka, E. and Lamb, M. J. (2014) *Evolution in Four Dimensions* 2nd edn (1st edn 2005) (Cambridge, MA).

Jackendoff, R. (1996) 'How language helps us think', *Pragmatics and Cognition* 4: 1–34.

James, W. (1902) *The Varieties of Religious Experience* (London).

Jarvie, I. C. (1983) 'Rationality and relativism', *British Journal of Sociology* 34: 44–60.

Jaspers, K. (1953) *The Origin and Goal of History* (trans. by M. Bullock of *Vom Ursprung und Ziel der Geschichte*, Munich, 1949) (London).

Jaynes, J. (1976) *The Origin of Consciousness in the Breakdown of the Bicameral Mind* (Boston, MA.).

Johnson-Laird, P. N. (2006) *How We Reason* (Oxford).

Johnston, I. (2010) *The Mozi* (Hong Kong).

Kahn, C. H. (1973) *The Verb 'Be' in Ancient Greek*, Foundations of Language Suppl. 16 (Dordrecht).

Kahneman, D. (2011) *Thinking Fast and Slow* (London).

Kahneman, D., Slovic, P. and Tversky, A. (eds.) (1982) *Judgment under Uncertainty: Heuristics and Biases* (Cambridge).

Karlgren, B. (1950) 'The Book of Documents', *Bulletin of the Museum of Far Eastern Antiquities* 22: 1–81.

Kennedy, A. (1984) *The Psychology of Reading* (London).

Kirk, G. S. (1970) *Myth: Its Meaning and Function in Ancient and Other Cultures* (Berkeley).

Knoblock, J. (1988–94) *Xunzi: A Translation and Study of the Complete Works*, 3 vols. (Stanford).

Knoblock, J. and Riegel, J. (2000) *The Annals of Lü Buwei* (Stanford).

Kroeber, A. L. and Kluckhohn, C. (1952) *Culture: A Critical Review of Concepts and Definitions*, Peabody Museum of American Archaeology and Ethnology 47 (Cambridge, MA).

Kuhn, T. S. (1970) *The Structure of Scientific Revolutions*, 2nd edn (1st edn 1962) (Chicago).

Kuhn, T. S. (1977) *The Essential Tension* (Chicago).

Kummer, H. (1995) 'Causal knowledge in animals', in Sperber, Premack and Premack (1995), pp. 26–36.

Kuper, A. (1999) *Culture: The Anthropologists' Account* (Cambridge, MA).

Kuriyama, S. (1999) *The Expressiveness of the Body and the Divergence of Greek and Chinese Medicine* (New York).

Lakatos, I. (1978) *The Methodology of Scientific Research Programmes: Philosophical Papers*, vol. 1, ed. J. Worrall and G. Currie (Cambridge).

Lambert, W. G. (1960) *Babylonian Wisdom Literature* (Oxford).

Lang, P. (ed.) (2004) *Reinventions: Essays on Hellenistic and Early Roman Science* (Kelowna).

Latour, B. (2013) *An Inquiry into Modes of Existence* (trans. by C. Porter of *Enquête sur les modes d'existence*, Paris, 2012) (Cambridge, MA).

Lave, J. (1988) *Cognition in Practice: Mind, Mathematics and Culture in Everyday Life* (Cambridge).

Lear, J. (1982) 'Aristotle's philosophy of mathematics', *Philosophical Review* 91: 161–92.

Leavitt, J. (2011) *Linguistic Relativities: Language Diversity and Modern Thought* (Cambridge).

Le Blanc, C. and Matthieu, R. (eds.) (2003) *Philosophes taoïstes II Huainan Zi* (Paris).

Levinson, S. C. (2005) 'Comments on Everett (2005)', *Current Anthropology* 46: 637–8.

Levinson, S. C. and Jaisson, P. (eds.) (2006) *Evolution and Culture* (Cambridge, MA).

Lévi-Strauss, C. (1966) *The Savage Mind* (trans. of *La pensée sauvage*, Paris, 1962) (London).

Lévi-Strauss, C. (1968) *Structural Anthropology* (trans. by C. Jacobson and B. G. Schoepf of *Anthropologie structurale*, Paris, 1958) (London).

Lévi-Strauss, C. (1969) *The Elementary Structures of Kinship* (revised edn) (trans. by J. H. Bell, J. H. von Sturmer and R. Needham of *Les structures élémentaires de la parenté*, Paris, 1949) (Boston).

Lévi-Strauss, C. (1970–81) *Introduction to the Science of Mythology* (trans. by J. and D. Weightman of *Mythologiques*, Paris, 1964–71) 4 vols. (London).

Lévy-Bruhl, L. (1923) *Primitive Mentality* (trans. by L. A. Clare of *La mentalité primitive*, Paris, 1922) (New York).

Li, X. A. (2015) *Comparative Encounters between Artaud, Michaux and the Zhuangzi: Rationality, Cosmology and Ethics* (London).

Lloyd, G. E. R. (1966) *Polarity and Analogy* (Cambridge).

Lloyd, G. E. R. (1979) *Magic, Reason and Experience* (Cambridge).

Lloyd, G. E. R. (1990) *Demystifying Mentalities* (Cambridge).

Lloyd, G. E. R. (1991) *Methods and Problems in Greek Science* (Cambridge).

Lloyd, G. E. R. (1996a) *Adversaries and Authorities* (Cambridge).

Lloyd, G. E. R. (1996b) *Aristotelian Explorations* (Cambridge).

Lloyd, G. E. R. (2000) 'On the "origins" of science', *Proceedings of the British Academy*, 105: 1–16.

Lloyd, G. E. R. (2002) *The Ambitions of Curiosity* (Cambridge).

Lloyd, G. E. R. (2003) *In the Grip of Disease: Studies in the Greek Imagination* (Oxford).

Lloyd, G. E. R. (2005) 'The institutions of censure: China, Greece and the modern world', *Quaderni di Storia* 62: 7–52.

Lloyd, G. E. R. (2006) *Principles and Practices in Ancient Greek and Chinese Science* (Aldershot).

Lloyd, G. E. R. (2007a) *Cognitive Variations: Reflections on the Unity and Diversity of the Human Mind* (Oxford).

Lloyd, G. E. R. (2007b) 'The wife of Philinus, or the doctors' dilemma: medical signs and cases and non-deductive inference', in D. Scott (ed.), *Maieusis* (Oxford), pp. 335–50.

Lloyd, G. E. R. (2009) *Disciplines in the Making* (Oxford).

Lloyd, G. E. R. (2012a) *Being, Humanity, and Understanding* (Oxford).

Lloyd, G. E. R. (2012b) 'The pluralism of Greek "mathematics"', in Chemla (2012b), pp. 294–310.

Lloyd, G. E. R. (2013) 'Aristotle on the natural sociability, skills and intelligence of animals', in V. Harte and M. Lane (eds.), *Politeia in Greek and Roman Philosophy* (Cambridge), pp. 277–93.

Lloyd, G. E. R. (2014) *The Ideals of Inquiry* (Oxford).

Lloyd, G. E. R. (2015) *Analogical Investigations* (Cambridge).

Lloyd, G. E. R. and Sivin, N. (2002) *The Way and the Word* (New Haven).

Lloyd-Jones, H. (1983) *The Justice of Zeus*, 2nd edn (1st edn 1971) (Berkeley).

Long, A. A. and Sedley, D. N. (1987) *The Hellenistic Philosophers*, 2 vols. (Cambridge).

Luhrmann, T. (2012) *When God Talks Back: Understanding the American Evangelical Relationship with God* (New York).

Lukes, S. (2000) 'Different cultures, different rationalities?', *History of the Human Sciences* 13, 1: 3–18.

Luria, A. R. (1976) *Cognitive Development: Its Cultural and Social Foundations* (Cambridge, MA).

McGilchrist, I. (2009) *The Master and His Emissary: The Divided Brain and the Making of the Western World* (New Haven).

McGrew, W. C. (1992) *Chimpanzee Material Culture* (Cambridge).

McKirahan, R. D. (1992) *Principles and Proofs: Aristotle's Theory of Demonstrative Science* (Princeton).

Major, J. S. (1993) *Heaven and Earth in Early Han Thought* (Albany, NY).

Major, J. S., Queen, S. A., Meyer, A. S. and Roth, A. D. (eds.) (2010) *The Huainanzi: A Guide to the Theory and Practice of Government in Early Han China* (New York).

Malinowski, B. (1925) 'Magic science and religion', in J. Needham (ed.), *Science, Religion and Reality* (London), pp. 19–84.

Markus, H. R. and Kitayama, S. (1991) 'Culture and the self: implications for cognition, emotion, and motivation', *Psychological Review* 98: 224–53.

Martzloff, J.-C. (2006) *A History of Chinese Mathematics* (trans. by S. S. Wilson of *Histoire des mathématiques chinoises*, Paris, 1988) 2nd edn (Berlin).

Martzloff, J.-C. (2009) *Le calendrier chinois: structure et calculs (104 av. J.C. – 1644)* (Paris).

Matilal, B. K. (1985) *Logic, Language and Reality: An Introduction to Indian Philosophical Studies* (Delhi).

Matilal, B. K. (1998) *The Character of Logic in India* (ed. J. Ganeri and H. Tiwari) (Albany, NY).

Matthews, G. B. (1984) *Dialogues with Children* (Cambridge, MA).

Matthews, G. B. (1994) *The Philosophy of Childhood* (Cambridge, MA).

Medin, D. L. and Atran, S. (eds.) (1999) *Folkbiology* (Cambridge, MA).

Mercier, H. (2011) 'On the universality of argumentative reasoning', *Journal of Cognition and Culture* 11, 85–113.

Mercier, H. and Sperber, D. (2011) 'Why do humans reason? Arguments for an argumentative theory', *Behavioral and Brain Sciences* 34, 57–74.

Mercier, H. and Sperber, D. (2017) *The Enigma of Reason: A New Theory of Human Understanding* (London).

Merton, R. K. (1938) *Science, Technology and Society in Seventeenth-Century England* (New York).

Merton, R. K. (1973) *The Sociology of Science* (Chicago).

Meyer, B. (2016) 'How to capture the "wow": R. R. Marett's notion of awe and the study of religion', *Journal of the Royal Anthropological Institute* 22: 7–26.

Mohanty, J. N. (1992) *Reason and Tradition in Indian Thought* (Oxford).

Mourelatos, A. P. D. (1980) 'Plato's "real astronomy", *Republic* 527d–531d', in Anton (1980), pp. 33–73.

Mourelatos, A. P. D. (1981) 'Astronomy and kinematics in Plato's project of rationalist explanation', *Studies in History and Philosophy of Science* 12, 1: 1–32.

Mueller, I. (1980) 'Ascending to problems: astronomy and harmonics in Plato's *Republic*', in Anton (1980), pp. 103–21.

Needham, J. (1956) *Science and Civilisation in China,* vol. 2, *History of Scientific Thought* (Cambridge).

Needham, J. (1978) 'Address to the opening session of the XV International Congress of the History of Science, Edinburgh, 11 August 1977', *British Journal for the History of Science* 11.2: 103–113.

Netz, R. (1999) *The Shaping of Deduction in Greek Mathematics* (Cambridge).

Netz, R. (2009) *Ludic Proof* (Cambridge).

Nickerson, R. S. (1998) 'Confirmation bias: a ubiquitous phenomenon in many guises', *Review of General Psychology* 2: 175–220.

Nickerson, R. S. (2008) *Aspects of Rationality* (New York).

Nielsen, K. (1974) 'Rationality and relativism', *Philosophy of the Social Sciences* 4: 313–31.

Nisbett, R. E. (2003) *The Geography of Thought: How Asians and Westerners Think Differently . . . and Why* (New York).

Nisbett, R. E. and Ross, L. (1980) *Human Inference: Strategies and Shortcomings of Social Judgement* (Englewood Cliffs, NJ).

Norenzayan, A. (2013) *Big Gods: How Religion Transformed Cooperation and Conflict* (Princeton).

Nutton, V. (2004) *Ancient Medicine* (London).

Nylan, M. (2001) *The Five 'Confucian' Classics* (New Haven, CT).

Nylan, M. and Sivin, N. (1995) 'The first Neo-Confucianism: an introduction to Yang Hsiung's "Canon of Supreme Mystery" (*T'ai hsuan ching*, ca. 4 B.C.)', revised edn (originally 1987) in Sivin (1995a): Chapter III.

Ober, J. (1989) *Mass and Elite in Democratic Athens* (Princeton).

Olivelle, P. (1996) *Upaniṣads* (Oxford).

Olson, D. R. (1994) *The World on Paper* (Cambridge).

Olson, D. R. and Torrance, N. (eds.) (1991) *Literacy and Orality* (Cambridge).

Olson, D. R. and Torrance, N. (eds.) (1996) *Modes of Thought: Explorations in Culture and Cognition* (Cambridge).

Ong, W. J. (1977) *Interfaces of the Word: Studies in the Evolution of Consciousness and Culture* (Ithaca).

Ong, W. J. (1982) *Orality and Literacy* (London).

Onians, R. B. (1951) *The Origins of European Thought* (Cambridge).

Osborne, C. (2007) *Dumb Beasts and Dead Philosophers. Humanity and the Humane in Ancient Philosophy and Literature* (Oxford).

Osborne, R. (1997) 'The polis and its culture', in C. C. W. Taylor (ed.), *From the Beginning to Plato: Routledge History of Philosophy,* vol. 1 (London), pp. 9–46.

Osborne, R. (2010) *Athens and Athenian Democracy* (Cambridge).

Owen, G. E. L. (1986) *Logic, Science and Dialectic* (London).

Padel, R. (1992) *In and Out of the Mind* (Princeton).

Parry, J. P. (1985) 'The Brahmanical Tradition and the Technology of the Intellect', in J. Overing (ed.), *Reason and Morality* (London), pp. 200–25.

Piaget, J. (1929) *The Child's Conception of the World* (trans. by J. and A. Tomlinson of *La représentation du monde chez l'enfant*, Paris, 1926) (London).

Piaget, J. (1930) *The Child's Conception of Physical Causality* (trans. by M. Gabain of *La causalité physique chez l'enfant*, Paris, 1927) (London).

Piaget, J. (1959) *The Language and Thought of the Child* (revised edn) (trans. by M. Gabain of *Le langage et la pensée chez l'enfant*, Paris, 1923) (London).

Pinker, S. (1997) *How the Mind Works* (London).

Prets, E. (2000) 'Theories of debate, proof and counter-proof in the early Indian dialectical tradition', Studia Indologiczne 7, in Piotr Balcerowicz and M. Mejor (eds.), *On the Understanding of Other Cultures* (Warsaw), pp. 369–82.

Prets, E. (2001) 'Futile and false rejoinders, sophistical arguments and early Indian logic', *Journal of Indian Philosophy* 29: 545–58.

Prets, E. (2003) 'Parley, reason and rejoinder', *Journal of Indian Philosophy* 31: 271–83.

Puett, M. J. (2001) *The Ambivalence of Creation: Debates Concerning Innovation and Artifice in Early China* (Stanford).

Puett, M. J. (2002) *To Become a God: Cosmology, Sacrifice, and Self-Divinization in Early China* (Cambridge, MA).

Puett, M. J. (forthcoming) 'Genealogies of gods, ghosts and humans', in G. E. R. Lloyd and J. Zhao (eds.), *Ancient Greece and China Compared* (Cambridge), pp. 160–86.

Putnam, H. (1981) *Reason, Truth and History* (Cambridge).

Quine, W. van O. (1960) *Word and Object* (Cambridge, MA).

Quine, W. van O. (1969) *Ontological Relativity and Other Essays* (New York).

Rappaport, R. A. (1999) *Ritual and Religion in the Making of Humanity* (Cambridge).

Rayner, K. and Pollatsek, A. (eds.) (1989) *The Psychology of Reading* (Englewood Cliffs, NJ).

Reding, J.-P. (1985) *Les fondements philosophiques de la rhétorique chez les sophistes grecs et chez les sophistes chinois* (Bern).

Regenbogen, O. (1930–1) *Eine Forschungsmethode antiker Naturwissenschaft*, Quellen und Studien zur Geschichte der Mathematik, Astronomie und Physik B 1.2 (Berlin), pp. 131–82.

Rips, L. J. (1998) *The Psychology of Proof: Deductive Reasoning in Human Thinking* (Cambridge, MA).

Robinson, R. (1953) *Plato's Earlier Dialectic*, 2nd edn (1st edn 1941) (Oxford).

Rochberg, F. (2004) *The Heavenly Writing: Divination, Horoscopy and Astronomy in Mesopotamian Culture* (Cambridge).

Rochberg, F. (2016) *Before Nature: Cuneiform Knowledge and the History of Science* (Chicago).

Rome, A. (1931) *Commentaires de Pappus et de Théon d'Alexandrie sur l'Almageste*, vol. 1, Pappus d'Alexandrie (Rome).

Rozin, P., Poritsky, S. and Sotsky, R. (1971) 'American children with reading problems can easily learn to read English represented by Chinese characters', *Science* 171: 1264–7.

Runciman, W. G. (2009) *The Theory of Cultural and Social Selection* (Cambridge).

Runciman, W. G., Maynard Smith, J. and Dunbar, R. I. M. (eds.) (1996) *Evolution of Social Behaviour Patterns in Primates and Man*, Proceedings of the British Academy 88 (Oxford).

Sahlins, M. (1995) *How 'Natives' Think, about Captain Cook, for Example* (Chicago).

Sakamoto, T. and Makita, K. (1973) 'Japan', in J. Downing (ed.), *Comparative Reading: Cross-National Studies of Behavior and Processes in Reading and Writing* (New York), pp. 440–65.

Sambursky, S. (1962) *The Physical World of Late Antiquity* (London).

Sambursky, S. (1965) 'Plato, Proclus, and the limitations of science', *Journal of the History of Philosophy* 3: 1–11.

Sapir, E. (1949) *Selected Writings of Edward Sapir in Language, Culture, and Personality* (Berkeley).

Schaberg, D. (1997) 'Remonstrance in Eastern Zhou historiography', *Early China* 22: 133–79.

Scheidel, W. (2004) 'Ancient Egyptian sibling marriage and the Westermarck effect', in A. Wolf and W. Durham (eds.), *Inbreeding, Incest, and the Incest Taboo: The State of Knowledge at the Turn of the Century* (Stanford), pp. 93–108.

Searle, J. (2001) *Rationality in Action* (Cambridge, MA).

Sedley, D. N. (2007) *Creationism and Its Critics in Antiquity* (Berkeley).

Severi, C. (2013) 'Philosophies without ontology', *HAU: Journal of Ethnographic Theory* 3: 192–6.

Severi, C. (2015) *The Chimera Principle: An Anthropology of Memory and Imagination* (trans. by J. Lloyd of *Le principe de la chimère: Une anthropologie de la mémoire*, Paris, 2007) (Chicago).

Seyfarth, R. M. and Cheney, D. L. (1982) 'How monkeys see the world: a review of recent research on East African vervet monkeys', in C. T. Snowdon, C. H. Brown and M. R. Petersen (eds.), *Primate Communication* (Cambridge), pp. 239–52.

Shapin, S. and Schaffer, S. (1985) *Leviathan and the Air-Pump: Hobbes, Boyle, and the Experimental Life* (Princeton).

Shaughnessy, E. L. (1997) *I Ching: The Classic of Changes* (New York).

Sivin, N. (1987) *Traditional Medicine in Contemporary China* (Ann Arbor).

Sivin, N. (1995a) *Medicine, Philosophy and Religion in Ancient China: Researches and Reflections*, vol. 2 (Aldershot).

Sivin, N. (1995b) *Science in Ancient China: Researches and Reflections*, vol. 1 (Aldershot).

Sivin, N. (1995c) 'Text and experience in classical Chinese medicine', in D. Bates (ed.), *Knowledge and the Scholarly Medical Traditions* (Cambridge), pp. 177–204.

Skinner, Q. (1966) 'The limits of historical explanations', *Philosophy* 41: 199–215.

Skinner, Q. (1969) 'Meaning and understanding in the history of ideas', *History and Theory* 8: 3–53.

Skinner, Q. (1971) 'On performing and explaining linguistic actions', *Philosophical Quarterly* 21: 1–21.

Skinner, Q. (1975) 'Hermeneutics and the role of history', *New Literary History* 7: 209–32.

Skoyles, J. (1984) 'Alphabet and the Western mind', *Nature* 309 (5967): 409–10.

Smith, A. M. (1982) 'Ptolemy's search for a law of refraction: a case-study in the classical methodology of "saving the appearances" and its limitations', *Archive for History of Exact Sciences* 26: 221–40.

Snell, B. (1953) *The Discovery of the Mind* (trans. by T. G. Rosenmeyer of *Die Entdeckung des Geistes*, 2nd edn, Hamburg, 1948) (Oxford).

Sorabji, R. (1993) *Animal Minds and Human Morals* (London).

Sperber, D. (1985) *On Anthropological Knowledge* (Cambridge).

Sperber, D., Cara, F. and Girotto, V. (1995) 'Relevance theory explains the selection task', *Cognition* 57: 31–95.

Sperber, D., Premack, D. and Premack, A. J. (eds.) (1995) *Causal Cognition: A Multidisciplinary Debate* (Oxford).

Staden, H. von (1989) *Herophilus: The Art of Medicine in Early Alexandria* (Cambridge).

Sterckx, R. (2002) *The Animal and the Daemon in Early China* (Albany, NY).

Sternberg, R. J. and Kaufman, J. C. (eds.) (2001) *The Evolution of Intelligence* (Hillsdale, NJ).

Stich, S. P. (1985) 'Could man be an irrational animal? Some notes on the epistemology of rationality', *Synthèse* 64, 1: 115–35.

Strathern, M. (1980) 'No nature, no culture: the Hagen case', in C. P. MacCormack and M. Strathern (eds.), *Nature, Culture and Gender* (Cambridge), pp. 174–222.

Strathern, M. (1988) *The Gender of the Gift* (Berkeley).

Szabó, Á. (1978) *The Beginnings of Greek Mathematics* (trans. by A. M. Ungar of *Anfänge der griechischen Mathematik*, Vienna, 1969) (Budapest).

Tambiah, S. J. (1968) 'The magical power of words', *Man* NS 3: 175–208.

Tambiah, S. J. (1973) 'Form and meaning of magical acts: a point of view', in Horton and Finnegan (1973), pp. 199–229.

Tambiah, S. J. (1990) *Magic, Science, Religion and the Scope of Rationality* (Cambridge).

Taylor, A.-C. (2013) 'Distinguishing ontologies', *Hau* 3: 201–4.

Taylor, I. and Taylor, M. M. (1983) *The Psychology of Reading* (New York).

Teich, M. and Müller, M. (eds.) (2005) *Historia Magistra Vitae?*, Österreichische Zeitschrift für Geschichtswissenschaften, 16.2 (Innsbruck).

Thomas, K. (1971) *Religion and the Decline of Magic* (London).

Thomas, R. (1989) *Oral Tradition and Written Record in Classical Athens* (Cambridge).

Tomasello, M. (1999) *The Cultural Origins of Human Cognition* (Cambridge, MA).

Tooby, J. and Cosmides, L. (1989) 'Evolutionary psychology and the generation of culture: part I, theoretical considerations', *Ethology and Sociobiology* 10: 29–49.

Tooby, J. and Cosmides. L. (1990) 'The past explains the present: emotional adaptations and the structure of ancestral environments', *Ethology and Sociobiology* 11: 375–424.

Tooby, J. and Cosmides, L. (1992) 'The psychological foundations of culture', in Barkow, Cosmides and Tooby (1992), pp. 19–136.

Toomer, G. J. (1984) *Ptolemy's Almagest* (London).

Turner, T. (2009) 'The crisis of late structuralism, perspectivism and animism: rethinking culture, nature, spirit, and bodiliness', *Tipití: The Journal of the Society for the Anthropology of Lowland South America* 7, 1: 1–40.

Tversky, A. and Kahneman, D. (1982) 'Judgment under uncertainty: heuristics and biases', in Kahneman, Slovic, and Tversky (1982), pp. 3–21 (original publ. *Science*, 1974 NS 185: 1124–31).

Tybjerg, K. (2004) 'Hero of Alexandria's mechanical geometry', in Lang (2004), pp. 29–56.

Unschuld, P. U. (1985) *Medicine in China* (Berkeley).

Van der Eijk, P. J., Horstmanshoff, H. F. J. and Schrijvers, P. H. (eds.) (1995) *Ancient Medicine in Its Socio-cultural Context* (Amsterdam).

Vanderpool, E. (1970) *Ostracism at Athens* (Cincinnati).

Vilaça, A. (2010) *Strange Enemies: Indigenous Agency and Scenes of Encounters in Amazonia* (trans. by D. Rodgers of *Quem somos nós: Os Wari' encontram os brancos*, Rio de Janeiro, 2006) (Durham, NC).

Viveiros de Castro, E. (1998) 'Cosmological deixis and Amerindian perspectivism', *Journal of the Royal Anthropological Institute* NS 4: 469–88.

Viveiros de Castro, E. (2014) *Cannibal Metaphysics* (trans. by P. Skafish of *Métaphysiques cannibales*, Paris, 2009) (Minneapolis).

Viveiros de Castro, E. (2015) *The Relative Native: Essays on Indigenous Conceptual Worlds* (Chicago).

Vlastos, G. (1973) *Platonic Studies* (Princeton).

Volkov, A. (1996–7) 'The mathematical work of Zhao Youqin: remote surveying and the computation of π', *Taiwanese Journal for Philosophy and History of Science* 5, 1: 129–89.

Volkov, A. (1997) 'Zhao Youqin and his calculation of π', *Historia Mathematica* 24: 301–31.

Vygotsky, L. (1986) *Thought and Language* (Cambridge MA).

Wagner, R. (2016) *The Invention of Culture*, 2nd edn (1st edn 1975) (Chicago).

Wardhaugh, R. (2010) *An Introduction to Sociolinguistics*, 6th edn (Oxford).

Wardy, R. B. B. (2000) *Aristotle in China: Language, Categories and Translation* (Cambridge).

Wason, P. C. (1966) 'Reasoning', in B. M. Foss (ed.), *New Horizons in Psychology* (Harmondsworth), pp. 135–51.

Wason, P. C. (1968) 'Reasoning about a rule', *Quarterly Journal of Experimental Psychology* 20: 273–81.

Wason, P. C. and Johnson-Laird, P. N. (1972) *Psychology of Reasoning: Structure and Content* (London).

Wasserstein, A. (1962) 'Greek scientific thought', *Proceedings of the Cambridge Philological Society* 188, NS 8: 51–63.

Watson, B. (2003) *Han Feizi: Basic Writings*, 2nd edn (1st edn 1964) (New York).

Watson, R. and Horowitz, W. (2011) *Writing Science before the Greeks* (Leiden).

Weber, M. (1930) *The Protestant Ethic and the Spirit of Capitalism*, trans. Talcott Parsons (London).

Weber, M. (1948) *From Max Weber: Essays in Sociology* (trans., ed. and intro. H. H. Gerth and C. Wright Mills) (London).

Whiten, A. and Byrne, R. W. (eds.) (1997) *Machiavellian Intelligence II* (Cambridge).

Whorf, B. L. (2012) *Language, Thought, and Reality*, 2nd edn, ed. J. Carroll, S. C. Levinson and P. Lee (1st edn 1956) (Cambridge, MA).

Wilson, B. R. (ed.) (1970) *Rationality* (Oxford).

Wittgenstein, L. (1953) *Philosophical Investigations*, trans. G. E. M. Anscombe (Oxford).

Wright, L. (1973–4) 'The astronomy of Eudoxus: geometry or physics?' *Studies in History and Philosophy of Science* 4, 2: 165–72.

Ziporyn, B. (2009) *Zhuangzi: The Essential Writings* (Indianapolis).

Index